Race and the Gospel

Race and the Gospel

Toward a Biblical Anthropology and Christian Humility

JASON TACKETT

WIPF & STOCK · Eugene, Oregon

RACE AND THE GOSPEL
Toward a Biblical Anthropology and Christian Humility

Wipf & Stock
An Imprint of Wipf and Stock Publishers
199 W. 8th Ave., Suite 3
Eugene, OR 97401

www.wipfandstock.com

PAPERBACK ISBN: 979-8-3852-7652-3
HARDCOVER ISBN: 979-8-3852-7653-0
EBOOK ISBN: 979-8-3852-7654-7

All Scripture references use the King James Version of the Bible.

Unless otherwise indicated, all italics in Scripture citations are added by the author.

Contents

Author's Preface

THOUGH THIS MAY DISAPPOINT some readers, the following is not a work of political theory. Having studied the issue of race, there is a common difficulty in separating race from politics and governance. As the camera changes the behavior of the one it points at, politics is performative and keeps people from speaking of race objectively and with clarity. Far too often the personal exercise of political speech amounts to nothing more than social exhibitionism, usually by those who have no ability to effect any political outcome. They produce nothing in their fervor except a litany of unintended consequences. I desire to avoid such pitfalls. The far more important question for the believer, if they wish like Paul to be separated unto the gospel (Rom 1:1), is how the subject of race relates to the gospel of Jesus Christ and not how it relates to the perceived political weal.

Therefore, this work is not intended to speak to important functions of government, security, and justice. No doubt it is the purpose of governments among men to establish just laws in accordance with the truth of God and to administer that justice accordingly. The duty of kings is to administer justice without partiality, giving justice to the poor when they are in the right. They must punish the evildoer regardless of their status and vindicate the righteous regardless of theirs. No doubt it is the duty of governors and kings to secure their citizens from enemies and maintain peace for their citizens. In doing so, they must recognize the existence of enemies and ensure the gates of the cities are secured against them. Any king that will not set watchmen on the wall is a traitor to his duty before God.

If anything said in this work appears to challenge a particular application of such principles, the fault either lies in the author's ability to properly apply the Scriptures or possibly in the reader's own political commitments in conforming to the Scriptures. Here then I pray that the reader will be willing to entertain the possibility that a political theory may go further than the Scriptures would allow them to go and to be humble enough to submit to what God has said. We pray that our application of the truths of the Scriptures will correct all areas in our hearts not aligned to God's truth. The cause of Christ is greater than any kingdom of this earth and their time-limited existence. The gospel will still be preached long after our national interests have been made footnotes in history books.

Another reason to set aside our political lenses in dealing with the subject of race is our need for humility in matters of politics. It is far more difficult to trace in real time the hand of providence as it works in political and geopolitical matters than our boasts will admit. It has been rightly said that providence, like the Hebrew language, is meant to be read backwards. Our independent opinions on history, as well as our bold predictions of the future, often assume omniscience which we do not possess. It may be the will of God for Gideon to take up arms against Israel's captors in one instance and yet sin to resist the captivity of Babylon in another (Jer 37). It may also be God's will to exalt a Jephthah who is not recognized as belonging to the house over which he comes to rule (Judg 12:1–2), or His will to reject a Rehoboam who seems to have the right pedigree (1 Kgs 12:1–15). God is turning the hearts of kings as He wills, and He is moving borders as He wills (Dan 4). That does not mean that we do not try to correct the evil of kings. It only means that we may in our politics easily find ourselves on the wrong side of what God is doing due to our own sinful obstinacy and ignorance. I do not exercise myself in matters too great for me (Ps 131), but I speak rather on what God has said about how I am to view and treat my fellow man. Let the political matters be worked out by God who sovereignly rules in the kingdoms of men. Let not our pet political ideologies find themselves in opposition to God.

Of course, every Christian should be desirous to see their form of government and its laws more firmly rooted in biblical principles and truths. However, any convictions one has about governance eventually ends with wicked men bearing rule in whatever framework that happens to be. David was a man after God's own heart, but even in David's rule it was not safe for a righteous Uriah to live peacefully or serve faithfully. Communism, fascism, and constitutional republicanism all fail to keep evil men from seizing the reins of power. One can say that they will rule by the word of God, but without the Spirit of God to give them a heart of flesh, their rule can be as tyrannical and unjust as the most ruthless atheist. Do I believe that laws should reflect what God has said to be good and that leaders are answerable to the Lord to do right? Yes, and yes. Therefore, my small voice will busily advocate for the first and warn of the second. My vote will go to the one that says they will do right and will cease to go for them when I realize they are lying. Those consumed with the business of how we should govern ourselves are too often losing sight of the trees while trying to comprehend the forest. My neighbor is always before me, while the political waves ebb and flow.

The following then, as much as it is faithful to the Scriptures, does not contradict good governance. It does not bind kings from recognizing needed security from known enemies or bar them from taking necessary steps to protect their kingdom. However, if one's politics repeatedly causes them to deny mercy or justice from their neighbor in malicious ways, as is taught by sound biblical principles, deep fault lies with that person's politics.

As such, the subject of race creates an odd paradigm for navigating how far one may reach out in fellowship to those who hold erring ideas. There are some who hold racial errors that do not delimit my ability to still call them brothers in Christ. To them, I admit in humility that I still have much to learn, not only about this subject matter but about how I can hold differing convictions while remaining charitable. There are others that hold egregious errors that fundamentally skew the clear commandments of God and denigrate the integrity and personhood of their neighbor. These wickedly lift themselves up as superior to their fellow man in an obnoxious manner, much like the scribes in the days of Christ. To those, convictions about the truth of God demand only that I withdraw from table fellowship with them and call them to repentance. While little space is given in this work to advise on how to navigate dealing with those that err, I pray that whatever is said in these pages will better equip myself and the reader in doing so.

I have long feared that our rebellious, indecent, and godless society will eventually produce a pseudo-moral order that will conquer and subjugate its lawlessness. I figured that this new order would fill the vacuum of morality left by liberal disorder, and it would be applauded when it comes with violent force. As Dumas said of Robespierre and the Great Terror he helped unleash to the cheer of many, "[He] brought a king to the level of the guillotine."[1] What I did not anticipate fully was for it to be draped in Christianity, and in the name of Christ, to spew hatred en masse while calling for violent force. My naivete has been corrected by what I see parading in the

1. Dumas, *Count of Monte Cristo*, 54.

virtual spaces where ideas of force are emerging and gaining momentum. The failure of governments to do the work of punishing evil inevitably produced this. Nevertheless, what is being produced is in no way Christian. The problem then is how to be a Christian in the transition. How we correct and encourage those who name the name of Christ in this matter is of surpassing importance. Knowing the truth of a matter is the greatest guide in dealing with error. I therefore devote myself to the subject at hand and pray that the Lord will use it. How we live, act, and speak with our neighbor, our enemy, our brother, or with the stranger is the sole matter this treatise aims at answering. I commend it to you.

In Christ,
Jason Tackett
Author

PART 1

In Adam All Die

INTRODUCTION

"For who maketh thee to differ from another? And what hast thou that thou didst not receive? Now if thou didst receive it, why dost thou glory, as if thou hadst not received it?" 1 CORINTHIANS 4:7

What is race? (a working definition)—Race is a descriptive term regarding what God in His sovereign providential work does in making families, tribes, and nations to differ one from another as He uses those differences to work out His purposes in history for His own glory.

RACE IS UNDERSTANDABLY AN uncomfortable subject for all. The natural urge of fallen man is to seek to find something in which to boast, and if that cannot be found as an individual, then it will be projected onto something else. The next natural thing to do is to project one's personal pride on those who are most like us; to find in those similar to us, or those we fancy to be such, some great nobility that we can relate to. This is necessary to achieve the sought-after sense of superiority. Such pride is what needs to be torn down. Tearing down one's own racial idols is an iconoclastic work, but it is not for the sake of iconoclasm itself. Jeremiah was told to destroy and pull down, and then to build up and plant (Jer 1:10). We must deface the image of Adam, of which we are so fond, so we can rather be conformed to the image of Christ. Such is the goal, though the means are troubling. Adam is where all things die, and that includes our natural race. Adam is what we must plead with men to forsake. Christ is where all live (1 Cor 15:22). That is where we wish all to be. Knowing the difference is important.

With that in mind, one must be mindful of the damage that can be done when pulling up tares mixed with wheat. There is a place for cultural and familial heroes. There is a place for appropriate meritorious monuments to be built for the good of cultures, families, and nations. I have such familial heroes, and I have no intention of plucking those up. My father was a great man, and my national history has its share of great men and women who are worthy of laud and praise. When we lack those heroes, it does indeed create a moral vacuum and cultural instability which is contrary to thriving. Knowing my father anchored my understanding of who I am. Knowing my history stabilized me. As Adam is defaced, the achievements in this world and the outstanding characters that wrought them are not the point of that defacing. Trust in the things of Adam is the intended target. The idea that my worth and value is found in my racial connection is set for destruction. The assertion that my dignity comes from some superficial physical or biological trait needs to be toppled.

Being a part of a community or having communicable traits is neither heroic nor virtuous. Every culture has built their statues and few among those cultures ever shared the perceived virtue of those heroes. Racial pride is often built on the flimsy scaffolding of believing our own hype. What we call cultural achievements are likely individual or small group achievements that are appropriated by many without corresponding warrant. The one wearing the jersey in the stands cheering for their team somehow believes they share in the glory of the achievement, but they neither possessed the gifts nor put in the work that the true victor did. They simply believe that because they wear a copy of the uniform they share in the virtue. Honor, merit, and achievement are not synonyms for race and the pride it produces.

Racial pride in its projection too often smears the good achievements of our heroes with embellishments. For instance, not every colonist was like Washington, and Washington was not himself without flaw. A fallacious assumption is that such a hero did this great thing, and it was then typical of all who share similar traits to do that very thing. Fantasizing minds can create a cultural idol that is much different than reality. Heroic stories are told because, when those things occur, they are exceptional. If they were common, they would not be told. Not everyone in Troy was Hector. There was only one Hector. A belief in the "good old days" is often the idea that everyone in Troy must have had the same traits as Hector. We do that without considering that many weaknesses were there in Hector's time that led to the fall of Troy. Warren Wiersbe has been attributed with identifying the sentiment of those who believe in the good old days; they suffer from two great maladies, a faulty memory and wishful thinking. Most of our "race" was carried along by a few great men, and that is so with every tribe. The inevitable destruction of every Adamic culture lies in the truth that the heroes are exceptions and not the rule. "Though Noah, Daniel, and Job were in it, as I live, saith the Lord God, they shall deliver neither son nor daughter; they shall but deliver their own souls by their righteousness" (Ezek 14:20). America has never possessed enough exceptional characters to keep it from rotting from the inside like all other cultures.

In all honesty, the matter is even worse than that. Not only was Washington not the rule but the exception; he was also very flawed. No man is sufficient to make a god. We tell our stories of Hercules in vain. No man has ascended to heaven except the Son that came down from heaven (John 3:13). We must yet even see our heroes in the light of God and the Adamic principle. David was also an adulterer. We could approach this point as a thought experiment. What if every citizen was indeed like Hector? Would Troy still stand? It may have stood for that particular time of Greek assault, but not forever. There was yet enough folly and corruption in Hector's nature to bring the eventual ruin of Troy even beyond the heroism of that single time. After all, the fate of Troy was sealed when Hector was unable to withstand Achilles. Most of us have no trouble thinking very highly of ourselves, so let us make this thought experiment more personal. If the fate of a city rested on the faithfulness of the populace, which was made up of perfect copies of you, how long would that city stand? If any of us were truly honest we would admit that the city would crumble in due time. Even my greatest heroes have limits to what is and what is not laudable in them. All of Priam's race was doomed to perish even with the heroism of Hector and would have shared the same fate even if it was made up only of heroes like Hector.

So, as we delve into all men sharing that same Adamic and fallen nature, we do so in hope that there is still room for us to cherish merit and achievement, and to still be able to build statues of great men. Nevertheless, we do this without rose-colored glasses and with greater sobriety. To say that in Adam all die is simply to point out the great problem with all men, even our heroes.

This is not a plea for egalitarianism where all are the same and can never rise any higher. It is rather a plea that the flaw in all our natures is recognized for what it is: death working in us all. We are all in Adam. Every one of my heroes had flaws. My flaws are even greater. Every one of my heroes died, and so I die. There was no perfect immutable state of my lineage in the past and there is no final utopian future for my lineage in the future. Outside of Christ, there is no hope. In Adam all die.

CHAPTER 1

The Zeitgeist

"But if our gospel be hid, it is hid to them that are lost: In whom the god of this world hath blinded the minds of them which believe not."
2 CORINTHIANS 4:3–4

"Ye are of your father the devil, and the lusts of your father ye will do. He was a murderer from the beginning, and abode not in the truth, because there is no truth in him. When he speaketh a lie, he speaketh of his own: for he is a liar, and the father of it." JOHN 8:44

"And you hath he quickened, who were dead in trespasses and sin; Wherein in time past ye walked according to the course of this world, according to the prince of the power of the air, the spirit that now worketh in the children of disobedience." EPHESIANS 2:1–2

IT BEHOOVES US TO test the spirits that influence us to see if they truly are of God (1 John 4:1). It was this very need that first caused me to take up this study. One day I found myself sitting across the table from a man teaching doctrines held by the Aryan Nations (i.e., Christian Identity) who was intent on trying to recruit me ideologically. He leaned in from the table and said to me, "Don't you see what is happening to your people?" Even though I knew nothing about the movement he was attached to, and even though there were partial truths that were peppered throughout his arguments, I was pressed by the idea that there was an evil spirit speaking. The more I learned about his ideology and others that correspond to it, the more I saw the wisdom of God's injunction to test the spirits and see whether they are of God.

Just because some form of truth comes from someone's lips does not mean that it comes from a godly spirit. The woman with an evil spirit followed Paul and Silas declaring that the apostles were proclaiming the true God—a statement that was true (Acts 16:16–18). However, that woman was working against the truth of God and not for it. Satan deals in slightly distorted truths for his own ends. The devil appears as an angel of light and his ministers as ministers of righteousness (2 Cor 11:13–15). Satan actively blinds minds as the prince of this world, and the works that men do betray the spirit that begat them. The world is swayed by this spirit, and the whole world lies in this wickedness (1 John 5:19). The zeitgeist must be recognized.

The spirit of this age is steeped in an obsession with identity. It does not seem needful or important that objective reality or an attested voice of authority underpin this identity. One needs only to be convinced in the structures of their own mind that such and such a thing is true about themselves, and that is enough to proclaim such an identity and to force the circumstances around them to suit that conviction. All authority and evidence must lay on the Procrustean bed of their convictions and be chopped off if they do not fit. All the outside circumstances around them must be made to affirm and bolster the identity they chose for themselves. Their lives become a walking aesthetic of them living "their truth" and being what they believe themselves to be. Their identity, whatever it happens to be, becomes the most important aspect of their life.

The spirit of identity, whether it is individual or group identity, prevails in all things political and personal. What is meant here is not the idea that one needs to come to know who they are in relation to God, their Creator and Redeemer, but rather that they declare their distinction as a unique individual or as a unique group in relation to others among mankind. This type of identity proudly informs one's philosophy and one's theology. A proud identity becomes the hermeneutic by which they understand God, His work in history, His present work, and the end. This is true of current "gender identity" and is so with contemporary racial ideology. The struggle to proclaim some special status or identity for oneself is at the heart of a resurgence of racial animus.

The concept of race allows some to have an outward manifestation of their supposed favored position, tangible marks differing from others who lack those marks. In this interpretive framework, the Scriptures themselves cease to be something that shapes how reality is perceived, and every text becomes a pretext for asserting what one already believes about themselves and others (see chapter 2). Some read the Scriptures and without surprise find that they themselves are the chosen of God based on who they physically are. They conveniently find for themselves a special connection with God and His promises based on their biology, and not on Christ. From that point, they also begin to interpret others. Those that do not share in their identity are the Canaanites, or the seed of Cain, or the seed of the serpent (supposed racial doctrines often touted). Whatever the other may be, they do not share naturally in the same blessings of God. Confirmation bias pervades in any accidental study of Scripture. It supposedly shows them that their skin color or accidental ethnic origins connect them to a glorious end, while others have a lesser or even a malevolent end. The terms may change depending on the group dynamic, but the sentiment of their faith is always the same.

Identity based on Christ is not found in such terms. God has chosen or elected persons, but it was never because they were good or mighty. He chose the weak things in this world that we may not boast but glory only in Him. Even those who find themselves among such chosen people find that He rejects the proud (1 Cor 1:26–31; 10:1–13). Abraham was chosen as a person "as good as dead" among heathen nations (Heb 11:12–14). From Abraham sprang a nation that God chose to bless, not as one that is destined to sit above the rest but to be a source of blessing to the rest (Gen 12:1–3). The True Israel came to serve and not to be served. God purposed in them that the house of the Lord would be built and called the house of prayer for all nations (Isa 56:7). It was never about a single nation but all nations. It was not about a tiny strip of land, but it was about the new heavens and the new earth (Rev 21). However, some still believe that it is only about their single ethnic group, about their "blood" and their "soil."

If there is one thing postmodernism teaches us, it is that relativism and individualism are not enough. Individual identity is insufficient to give meaning outside of a sense of community. There exists in all a need to belong, a need to be a part of something bigger and more important than the individual self. The one who fancies himself to be a nonconformist inevitably groups himself with others that walk, talk, act, and dress the same as himself. The looking glass self is not only defining oneself based on the perception of others but the validation of self by that same means.

The tendency is to not only find one's identity and validation in the group, but also to develop a sense of in-group and out-group dynamics (i.e., that there are those that are with us and those who are not). Without this, there is no sense of distinctiveness. We naturally sort and categorize people on that basis. Identity and validation in the scheme of group dynamics produces an ethnocentricity whereby "superiority" of the in-group is proclaimed, whatever group-defining characteristic that happens to be. It could be as mundane as the way we part our hair. This behavior is so predictable that it has been described by sociologists in social identity theory. However, Scripture gives a different account of the corruption of our social nature. James tells us that wars and fighting (i.e., division) comes from the lust that wars in us (Jas 4:1–4). This is the truth denied by secular sociologists. There is no peace to the wicked. The constant conflict of in-group/out-group dynamics confirms this.

The color of one's skin or their nation of origin are often convenient characteristics for the social identity phenomenon to work itself out among sinful men. Borders are most often drawn by blood, and the turmoil is spurred by one or both parties assuming rights over the other. Chattel slavery was justified by a sense of natural superiority. Master race ideology is not limited to one single slice of history. It is always horrifying to think of how easily people fall into conformity to the cruel will of the in-group against the out-group. Nazis believed themselves, based on their racial and cultural characteristics, to be superior. Thus, political efforts were fervently made to keep themselves pure from other races, and they believed that they were meant to rule in the end. The demonized out-group was easily seen as the only prohibiting factor to the realization of their glorious end. The outworking of that ideology was left in the ruins of history for us to pour over and dissect in disbelief.

Religious beliefs are not immune to the sinful effects of the fall and often make up the underpinning of ideology that gives shape to it. The gods of old were tribal gods, and when the tribes warred it was their gods that went before them. Usually those gods, those dumb idols, were just outward manifestations of all the falsehoods that made the particular group feel that they were better than their enemies. Any victory was attributed to the superiority of their gods.

Seeing that our need for community flows from the nature of the triune God and being created in His image (see chapters 3 and 4), that sense of community works itself out in all of us. Fidelity to one's family is good, as is tribal commonwealth, and seeking the good of one's city. In man's polity there is needed wisdom for borders to be kept secure, common culture encouraged, and enemies to be recognized by leaders and kept at bay. These are not sinful ideologies in themselves, but necessary aspects of governance. Such a sense of community always must be weighed by greater revelatory truth and fidelity to God. It must also be taken into account that we are fallen, and our sense of community may be skewed by our sinfulness and by depraved ends that are not in line with the truth of God. There are legitimate applications of in-group/out-group dynamics as they are exercised by familial and political entities, as long as they are not absolutized contrary to God's word. It is only wise to seek the wisdom and truth of God on how best to apply those realities. There may be a sinful application of in-group/out-group dynamics, and that must be repented of if the truth of God has revealed it.

In the communion of the saints, what does the in-group/out-group dynamic look like when it is conformed to the truth of God? The new covenant documents define our in-group/out-group dynamic. The unseen reality is that of election: those whom the Father gave to the Son to save, those saved by Christ who will be raised to glory in the last days (John 6). We cannot with our eyes behold that reality perfectly and are left to judge from our fellowship who bears the fruit of that. They are, in our sight, any who come to Christ in repentance and faith. They are those who continue in that repentance and faith. It transcends all other possible boundaries. All who are born of God are our brothers and sisters in Christ, equally part of the body of Christ. All who meet those qualifications may rightly be called our brother within the covenant of Christ, part of that multitude that no man can number who have the testimony of Christ and are made kings and priests with Christ (Rev 4). These will come from every nation, kindred, tribe, and tongue.

There are other moral aspects of such dynamics that become the scope of this present matter. The Christian is not incumbent to only act morally toward their own in-group. The Christian is not of the world but are definitely in the world and must relate to the world in a manner becoming to Christ. There are questions about how we treat those in the out-group (those who are lost), how we handle those who claim to be part of the in-group but appear to bear no fruit (those who profess salvation), and how we treat one another (those who profess and bear fruit). These categories are all-encompassing in the realm of our real and potential relationships.

They spill into our families, our workplaces, our churches, our politics, and so on.

To concentrate on the spirit of our age, let us draw attention to sinful assertions for community in Christ's church. The spirit of our age works to separate men into opposing interest groups. It is doing the same work in dividing churches as it does in political movements. Cultural Marxism first divided humanity covetously into economic groups but later began to divide people based on racial, gendered, ethnic, and sexual interests. Cultural Marxism is an evil to be avoided and has created a great amount of hostility. It has not only captured culture at large but has produced counterculture movements that embrace the divisions it constructed. Conservative postmodernism[1] is of no greater moral value than its liberal counterpart, though it is more readily accepted by those maintaining a sense of orthodoxy. The evil of the extreme of one side of the pendulum is not rejected by the opposite evil in the extreme swing to the other side. In fact, one seems to perpetuate the other. The appearance of a moral high ground is an illusion. Just because one swings their fists at evil ideologies does not make them righteous. Just because Hitler's regime championed a fight against pornographic materials and encouraged the nuclear family did not negate their evil Aryan vision for humanity. The latter was unchristian and contrary to the new covenant just as much as the former and has no place among the people of God.

It appears to become increasingly popular to define the in-group and out-group in ways that are not congruent with the new covenant but are rather congruent with modern identity politics (whether politics of the Left or Right). This is not unique to any specific demographic. One demands that the voices of one demographic be lifted above the other. Another says that preference should be given toward one's own racially defined demographic. One champions the perceived victim, or underdog. The other roots for the perceived winner. Each is equally convinced that the greatness of their group is hindered by the presence of the other.

As skin color often becomes the emerging topic in any discussion of race, it is convenient to embark from there. Here is one group that defines the in-group as being made up of those with darker skin. It seems benign at first. The claim may go something like this:

1. Postmodernism in this context means any view that sees communities emerging with their own separate truth narratives in hostility with other communities and their truth narratives.

- The true chosen people of God, the Israelite, had darker skin and the Ethiopian tribes bear that characteristic, therefore those with black skin are the chosen people of God.
- [Or] Solomon had a relationship with the Queen of Sheba and from that came the true chosen people of God who would inherit all the promises of God's covenants.[2]

It is not important that there be a demonstrable historical heredity or full biblical support for these assertions. What is important is that they have a text from which they can assert a presupposed faith claim (i.e., Israel is God's chosen people, therefore we are Israel). Some form of gnostic-like realization of their status as a true member of the true people of God based on genetic and ethnic characteristics can begin to take shape by faith. They can now have pride that they are the true people of God, based on their skin color instead of faith in Christ and repentance toward God.

Similar claims can be made on the other side of the spectrum. One such claim came to me from a Christian Identity group (one affiliated with the same one mentioned above):

> Anglo-Saxon, Germanic, Scandinavian, and kindred peoples [i.e., White Europeans] are the only people that fulfill all the prophetic identification marks as . . . God's covenant people.[3]

The in-group is so defined. Whether such statements have any true value is a broader discussion to be examined under different headings. For the sake of the argument alone, let us pretend that they do have some truth value. It is not truth that comes from Scripture but is at best extrabiblical in its reliance on outside historical research and opinion. It is not the faith once handed down to the saints or accessible to all. Therefore, to quote one friend on this subject, "So what?" If it were true, it would be a faith only for a few—unlike the gospel that goes everywhere.

The insidious nature of such statements is not their face value but the fruit they bear. There is something benign about one who believes that he is Napoleon. Malignity is found in this identity if others are demanded to submit to their superiority as Napoleon. What do such statements about

2. Common claims made by groups such as the Black Hebrew Israelites.

3. This is a paraphrase from a "statement of faith" of a group affiliated with Christian Identity and is also a central belief of all Christian Identity groups. Note: Christian Identity groups attempt to synthesize Neo-Nazi belief systems with Christianity. For more an in-depth analysis, see Goodrick-Clarke, *Black Sun*.

the abounding dignity of the in-group bring forth? To speak in a Hegelian manner, in creating the thesis an immediate antithesis is brought forth. The in-group creates an identity for the out-group. By consequence, they create a destiny with that identity. The in-group holds some form of "superiority" and the out-group, at the very least, is made to occupy some form of "inferiority." You cannot define the in-group without saying something contrary about the out-group. Moreover, if you start with a mistaken view of who the in-group is, you can only be in error about the nature of the out-group.

Based solely on the providence of their ethnic and tribal identities, the out-group in such schemes is made to take a position beneath the in-group. The former tribal gods return with their claims of superiority. The inferior position of the out-group may result in a malevolent end, a boot on the neck or chains of slavery. The inferior position may also be some form of perceived benevolent subordination. The out-group is not the victor but in a lesser way benefits from the victor. Ultimately, the out-group is less the subject of grace in the mind of the supremacist, and when such definitions are attained through a speculative biblical and historical hermeneutic as opposed to firm and objective revelation that is clearly accessible to any who have eyes to see and ears to hear, such conclusions can only be destructive spiritually and socially. They may stand on the streets and preach a gospel, but it is a false gospel that is only for certain "kinds" of people, at least in its fullness.

On the fringes of Christendom are a plethora of Christian Identity groups or Black Hebrew Israelite movements that hold such views. A quick read of any of their doctrinal statements is sufficient to see the pattern of doctrinal claims: ethnic superiority based on race, ecclesiastical segregation based on race, and eschatological ends varied due to race. The in-group is "in" based on race (and likely some gnostic form of initiation whereby their racial dignity/identity is openly embraced) and the out-group is "out" based on the same.

However, these divisions of humanity based on racial ideology have not remained on the fringes of Christendom, nourished by pseudo-historical hermeneutics. There are those that will eschew Christian Identity and Black Hebrew Israelism, maintaining a semblance of orthodoxy and doctrinal fidelity, and yet hold to similar ethnic views. With the influence of contemporary media, the most outrageous voices have garnered the attention and imagination of many in the visible church. Those who once proclaimed Christ in this world to all nations, under the pressure of these malicious and vain voices, have become proclaimers of the dignity of their own racial identity. These make racial politics the defining mark of their open ministries. The malicious voices have capitalized on the feeling of disfranchisement genuinely felt by many young men living under the constant maddening effects of Marxist depravity and its evil segmentation of society into warring classes. They have come to the sad conclusion that the only way to combat the Marxist fire is by adopting that evil segmentation with a fire of their own. The ministers of race move their devotees in their rhetoric as pupils being catechized from the seemingly benign to the overtly vicious (see chart below). The Overton window is subtly shifted to the "us-versus-them" paradigm. This is not an "us" and "them" that is defined in scriptural terms (With Christ/Against Christ—Righteous/Wicked). This is an "us" and "them" where the "us" are people who are physically similar and the "them" are not. The "them" are reduced to objects of wrath.

Progressive Catechizing Statements

"It is natural to love those that are like you."	**"We have a moral obligation to care about our heritage."**	**"I am just noticing the harmful trends in other races."**	**"It's not a sin to care more about my own people than other people."**	**"I want my children to have my heritage. I love my race."**	**"It's not a sin to say that I do not want my children to be around those people."**
"I do not hate anyone. I am just concerned about my heritage and my nation."	**"My racial heritage is superior."**	**"My race ought to be in charge. There ought to be an aristocracy."**	**"Those people should not have the same rights as we do."**	**"Those people should be expelled."**	**"Those people should be destroyed to save our own race."**

The validity of any given statement above on the earlier benign side is not being argued here. These are all real statements that are made repeatedly by members of the most vicious racist sects. They are also too often repeated by others claiming that they are saying them from a Christian perspective. The more benign statements lead to the more malignant when repeated often enough.

It does not take a prophetic word to see that our depraved and segmented society will open the door to a more vicious rule that promises to restore order. Every dystopian story has this similar element, and human history shows this to be an observable phenomenon. There is no reason to believe that this vicious spirit cannot come dressed in the garb of Christianity and that hatred of the other would include a desire to see a "Christian prince" to address the issue. The number of people presenting themselves as Christian and ministers of the gospel who spend the greater portion of their time declaring the dangers of "race mixing" and need for "heritage citizenship" is increasing.

There is a juvenile quality in much of their antics. Like the gnostics of old, they hide their true intent behind coded language which they believe to be for initiates only. It would be tedious here and contrary to the purpose of this work to attempt to cite the many instances of this. It would include invoking images of figures like George Lincoln Rockwell as representative of a Christian heritage,[4] repeatedly disseminating former Nazi and Neo-Nazi conspiratorial narratives regarding Jews and minorities, and Christianizing old Neo-Nazi symbols to secretly code their own movement. A recent example of the latter was exchanging David Lane's Fourteen Words (i.e., "We must secure the existence of our people and a future for white children")[5] with a Christianized Eleven Words (i.e., "White evangelicals are the lone bulwark against moral insanity in America"), and exchanging the symbol "88" with the "Christian" symbol "83."[6] "1183" was being used with a nod and wink by many in the "Christian nationalist" movement in their social media presence as late as the spring of 2025 (see footnote below).

All this rhetoric and use of symbols represent not just a political view but a spiritual division of the people of God. Those that use the symbols go about with their inside joke and become indignant when questioned about the connections those symbols invoke. How much they are willing to agree with Neo-Nazi rhetoric is left vague, and they go on slowly catechizing a generation of young men into believing more and more of their rhetoric. They do so without ever giving serious thought to what spirit is coming

4. A provocative and popular American Neo-Nazi from the 1950s and 1960s.

5. Michael, "David Lane and the Fourteen Words."

6. "1488" is a Neo-Nazi symbol—"14" refers to the fourteen words of the Neo-Nazi movement, David Lane's Fourteen Words. "88" is a symbol referring to the eighth letter of the alphabet consecutively, representing "Heil Hitler!" Sometimes, Neo-Nazis would use the symbol "18" to represent "Adolph Hitler." On social media platforms "Christian Nationalists" invoked the symbol "1183" where the Fourteen Words were replaced with the eleven words that were posted on the X platform by popular Christian Nationalist leader Stephen Wolfe. "83" replaced "88" as a "Christianized" version symbolizing the eighth and the third letter of the alphabet standing for "Heil Christ!" This is one of many examples of attempted synthesis between Neo-Nazism and the Christian faith.

from them, how their rhetoric affects their witness for Christ, or where it is going to end.

Revolutionary thought waits insidiously on an opportunity to synthesize itself with the opportune ideology. Christian thought is not immune to this reality. With the emergence of the New Left came also a Marxist synthesis with the Christian faith. It gave rise to liberation theology as an impetus for communist revolution in the 1970s, specifically in areas of Latin America. This synthesis is still at work in Left-leaning Christian fellowships regarding race (e.g., critical race theory) and relates itself to the same revolutionary ends. The same phenomenon is at work on the Right, but instead of synthesizing itself with communist utopian ends in its revolutionary work, it tries to bring Christian language to bear on National Socialist ends. It strives to make every Christian man a "Crusader" for a kingdom of this world that it calls "Christendom" and to bear a literal sword. It calls upon them to believe that the only way to "defend" their home or way of life is to drive out, subjugate, or even kill those people who are hindering those strong nationalist utopian ends.

At some point the spirit of all this must be examined in the light of the Scriptures and judged by God. There is presently something appealing to our flesh—to see ourselves and people like us as possessing some sort of superiority. At what point does our view of self turn into hurtful pride? We must ask ourselves if it is a pharisaical spirit working in us contrary to the word of God, a voice saying, "I thank God I am not like other people" (Luke 18:11).

CHAPTER 2

The Christian Metanarrative

"Sanctify them through thy truth: thy word is truth." JOHN 17:17

IT IS NOT THE intent of this work to mount a negative attack or act as a polemic against aberrant ideologies, though they of necessity will be identified. The work is rather intended to put forth a positive theology of race. Such would be far more edifying than simply attacking other structures. Let those ideologies simply be seen for what they are when compared to scriptural truth. Before raising a positive theological structure, solid ground must be sought for a foundation. To find that solid ground, some deep digging must be patiently done to locate the bedrock. This requires an examination of the weighty matters of methodology and epistemology prior to any assertions being made.

To begin with, we are Christian, and we do not leave the confines of our faith to speak about this matter of race. Let the atheist speak as an atheist. It cannot be otherwise. It is so with us as well. As Christians, our doctrinal conviction is not just that God has inspired the Scriptures, but that those Scriptures are sufficient for all faith and practice. As with all our faith, this conviction is not just a dusty doctrine that we assent to in our minds. It is a doctrine meant to be lived out in the world in all its fullness. Being the sole source of hearing the voice of God speaking, Scriptures are therefore the sole source of us knowing the will of God and then being equipped to do the will of God.

There is a practical relationship between the Scriptures and our usefulness for God in this wicked, brutal, and dark world where we are called upon as children of God to shine as lights (Matt 5:14–16; Phil 2:15). The Scriptures sanctify us in this present evil world. Paul told us that we are not to be conformed to this world, but rather to be transformed. What is the means of this transformation? We are to be "transformed by the renewing of [our] mind" (Rom 12:1–2). That is what enables us to offer ourselves to God wholly and rightly in this world. In reference to previous prophecy, Paul again says, "The righteousness of God [is] revealed from faith to faith: as it is written, the just shall live by faith" (Rom 1:17). What does that phrase "from faith to faith" mean? The righteousness we have in the gospel of Christ moves from the faith that we hear and believe to the faith that we practice and bring to fruition in our works in this world. That truth is summarized, "The just shall live." How will they live? They will live by means of faith. Is there another way for the just to live other than by faith? The Scriptures allow for none. The just will, in other words, live by hearing the voice of their Shepherd and following what they have heard in all things (John 10:27).

Paul in a similar vein wrote to the Corinthians, expounding on our coming glorification. He there gave a parenthetical statement about our life as it is lived out here and now. He says, "We walk by faith" (2 Cor 5:7). To walk (*peripateó*) speaks of conducting ourselves in a certain way. It is a complex word that contains a preposition (*peri*), giving it the quality of going around, connecting it to the entire circumference of our experience. As we go around, wherever we may go, we conduct ourselves by faith. There is no circumstance in life where our faith does not define us. Paul further told us how we do not conduct ourselves. We walk "not by sight." That is, we do not allow ourselves to be conducted in any way by our *eidos*—by *how we see things* either concretely or conceptually. This is a reiteration of what was taught by Solomon—that we lean not on our own understanding but rather trust in the Lord (Prov 3:5). Leaning on our own understanding is intuitively what we desire to do. There is a vast difference between the world as God sees it and declares it to be and how we see things. The world says, "I believe what I can see or touch, and I'm going by that. I'm going by these observations that I have and what is right in my own eyes." Building on such sand is folly. The Christian is rather to turn, hear the voice of God, and trust in that.

In the Thirty-Seventh and Seventy-Third Psalms the same pitfalls are shown for our example. The observations made in those psalms were in line with our own understanding that we too often lean upon—that moral wickedness prospers, and the righteous ones suffer. That is a good summary of the wicked world as observed by the eyes of fallible man. However, when revelation is believed it teaches something different. It teaches that the righteous ultimately are blessed and the meek shall inherit the earth. While it does not appear so right now, that is how things truly are when the world is seen through the eyes of faith. That should affect how the righteous live in the world.

In another place, Christ says, "It is written, Man shall not live by bread alone, but by every word that proceeds out of the mouth of God" (Matt 4:4). We go from faith being applied to all of life to faith being defined as all that God has said or breathed out. Here is our fundamental principle: the Scriptures are God speaking. All of what God has spoken to us shapes everything for us. It shapes how we view ourselves. It shapes how we view our friends. It shapes how we view our neighbors and how we view our enemies. It shapes how we view the created world, and it also shapes everything we do in it. We live by faith—by what has proceeded from His mouth (2 Tim 3:16).

The Great Commission also demonstrates the supremacy of Scripture to our living faith. It tells us to go into all the world, make disciples, and baptize. Then it tells us to teach those who follow Christ to observe and do all that Christ commands (Matt 28:18–20). In all things, we are not left to fumble around and figure things out on our own. *Sola scriptura* (i.e., "Scripture alone") is not a cerebral doctrine. There is no part of our thought life that it should not touch and should not rule over. It is an all-encompassing doctrine.

All that Christ has done on behalf of the believing sinner, the trusting sinner, flows faithfully from what God revealed by the apostles and prophets. The church is founded on the apostles and prophets who have Christ as the cornerstone of their foundation (Eph 2:20). We have a received faith that points to and emanates from the One who heaven has commanded, "Hear Him!" (Matt 17:5). This God-breathed truth can make us wise unto salvation and is able also to equip us wholly in this life to every possible good work (2 Tim 3:15–17). In it we have all things that pertain to life and godliness (2 Pet 3:3).

To our purpose, it is the Scriptures that speak of our life and the world in which it is found. In other words, it speaks with sole authority regarding our life in the flesh as it is lived in a physical and fallen world—a world which God created, made known, and has cursed due to man's disobedience. Scriptural authority is what is able to make us holy vessels for the Lord in that fallen and sinful world. It alone answers the question: How shall we then live? We live and walk in God's reality alone. We are sanctified in that reality by remaining in the confines of God's Word. Nothing else—no other voice—has the nature of the Scriptures. It is breathed out (or spoken) by God and alone is an infallible guide in the darkness of this world. If we were to ask, "What should I do now?" or "How shall I live overall?" we must turn to what God has said about the matter directly or in principle in order to live, act, or think rightly in each context. We have a sure starting point for everything.

All knowledge begins with the fearful revelation of God and our recognition of it. "The fear of the LORD *is* the beginning of knowledge: *but* fools despise wisdom and instruction" (Prov 1:7). The fool will not receive instruction, but those who fear God will. There is a stooping before God that precedes all true senses of knowing and that includes both the knowledge of ourselves and the knowledge of others.

The nature of revelation has always underpinned anything that man knows. What do we know about cosmology and metaphysics? By faith we know that the worlds were framed by God and made from nothing (Heb 11:1–3). We did not arrive at that thought through independent observation or deductive reasoning. God has been making Himself known from the moment He spoke, "Let there be . . ." We are presented with the created order and told by God that it is His created order. Man only named and took dominion over the creation that was presented to him by God (Gen 2:18–20). Neither do we arrive at human dignity in an independent manner. Revelation alone tells us that we are greater than dogs and are crowned by God (see chapter 4). Nature working without the revelation of God could tell us nothing of this, and all dominion work still flows from the same place. Purpose in life is a matter of faith in God and not the sight of our eyes. Moral reality is even more so. The first sin, for instance, was a transgression of revelation. Moral reality from Sabbath-keeping to murder has always been dependent on God speaking.[1] Without revelation, why should we not live the philosophy of the film *Natural Born Killers* (1994)? Animals are predators; why not men?

Creation is the voice of God having brought all things into being and defining their parameters. God alone reveals how that voice may be heard

1. I.e., God made known that He rested the seventh day from creation, made known that all human beings are made in the image of God, and that He alone gives life.

and interpreted. Nature is the voice of God and traces of His handiwork (Ps 19:1–6). What are the Scriptures in relation to that nature? They are that same voice of God interpreting the created order and declaring its meaning. Nature is read through the Scriptures prior to any study we give to it. It is dependent on what God has said, regardless of how often man claims its independence. One might wrongly say, "Grace does not destroy nature," but they say such as if nature had an independent authority outside the voice of God's interpretation. Nature glorifies God, and its voice is heard in every language (natural revelation). Nevertheless, what is that voice in a fallen world among sinful men who do not want to hear the voice of God? There is, as has been said, enough in nature to condemn all. God's eternal power and divinity are clearly seen, revealing His wrath against sin and sinners (Rom 1:18–20), but sinful men (as a product of their sinfulness and fallenness) exchange that truth for a lie and reverence all that is not God instead (Rom 1:21–28). Those who refuse to hear God speaking through the prophets will only go about fashioning idols out of the things they find in nature.

Much has been made about the concept of natural law and there is rarely agreement about what it is. In almost any discussion of race, someone's concept of natural law inevitably tries to take center stage. Faithful Christians most often speak about natural law in accordance with Scripture to which no rebuke is offered.[2] However, there are some that tout concepts of natural law in a way that denies the sufficiency of Scriptures to speak. That is, in given applications of knowledge (what we should believe about our neighbor, about morality in general, about politics, etc.), they set aside what the Scriptures say about that matter. They instead rely on the supposed equal light of their own reasoning (rationalism) or experience (empiricism). Too often this is a hard-and-fast methodological hermeneutic. In other words, they profess *themselves to be wise* and not in need of hearing what God has said to rightly reason on any given topic. Revelation, for such, only serves them if it helps support their own independent conceptions, and it is easily disregarded when it does not support those conceptions.

2. There is knowledge from nature. There is a Creator, and all know that the Creator is distinct from themselves and all other created things. That is, the Creator is not a creature. That same natural revelation shows man that they are under the wrath of an Almighty God, that they are living in a moral order. The Creator is angry with sinners, and all live under His wrath. We know this because we are given a conscience that tells us of our wrongs, and we act in community to create laws that reflect that we know there are things that are wrong and right to do.

Again, the grace of revelation (to them) cannot destroy or change nature as they have reasoned about it. They see their minds and their abilities as being untouched by sin and themselves as able to reason to a proper conclusion.

An example of this would be the fact that God has spoken on matters of anthropology and polity in the Scriptures, yet those that boast of "natural law" in an unbiblical sense will hold convictions on those matters without ever feeling that they need to refer to or be dependent on what God has said. What they believe about their neighbor is no longer informed by revelation but by their well-crafted syllogisms and inductive reasoning from their own observations. This becomes the sum of their faith in those particular matters.

As a brief rebuke to a revelation-independent utilization of natural law, one need only point out the imperfection of such tools and methodologies. If the ability of man to reason independently from empirical or conceptual observations could lead to certain truth on any given matter, then where is the infallible philosopher or school of philosophy? What about empiricism? Can we start with the phrase "I observe" from our own finiteness and make universal applications? Inductive reasoning, which underpins science, makes no such claim. At best, one may arrive at something that is "more probable" than its presently known alternatives, but it remains falsifiable if new information is considered. It never holds the status of truth. We may become certain that there is a force we call gravity, but we are never certain of the infallibility of the current theories that we use to describe it or its relationship to other phenomena.[3]

Morally, reliance on our own conceptions ignores a glaring reality—humans (fallen and sinful humans) are the ones doing science and philosophy. Human history shows us that sinful men usually find only what they look for. This is called confirmation bias, and it plagues every man with an inkling of self-interest. We interpret data based on what we already want that data to say. Mark Twain popularized the statement about three kinds of lies that he put in order of descending levels of viciousness: "[There are] lies, [vicious] lies, and statistics." That is, we tend to cherry-pick our observations to favor the conclusion we already desired to arrive at. Statistics rarely, if ever, speak for themselves. That is due to their finite nature. No set of statistics has ever accounted for all possible variables, known or unknown. That is why the weather report is never accurate in long-range predictions. Social sciences are even less accurate than the weather. We try

3. See Clark, *Philosophy of Science*.

to say what the measurements mean and usually make them say only what we want them to mean. Yet most conversations about race start and end with statistics (our limited observations).

For a Christian, conclusions can never be arrived at by rationalism or empiricism. Reality, framed by the word of God, is the necessary precondition for the believer, and therefore that faith is the starting point for all observation. God speaking is the position from which we reason outward. More importantly, we reason toward how we act in this world toward our fellow man from the Scriptures alone.

Here, then, is the glaring problem with revelation-independent reasoning—it must start and end with the world of our real experience. Without God speaking, what we reason from nature in its fallen state and must conclude is that it is brutal. In this, the atheist and Darwinist are far more consistent than many supposed Christian thinkers. We do not learn "love your neighbor as yourself" by watching nature "red in tooth and claw." The secular world reasons from nature in their sinfulness and concludes from that reasoning that all is "survival of the fittest." Let us give them credit here for their consistency. Evolutionary history seems to make sense based on a world under wrath, especially when you deny the moral reality of that wrath. The brutality observed by the secular mind trumps what the Christian claims if all things are considered equal. Paul admits as much when he says that if Christ is not raised all we do is vain, and we are the most miserable of all (1 Cor 15:1–20).

In the end of Tolstoy's *Anna Karenina*, the character Levin realized that his reasoning and science could not lead him to moral or metaphysical truth. At a time where he was in danger of following the same life pattern of the adulteress Anna (who in her unrepentant state saw all reality as a hateful mockery driving her to suicide), Levin said:

> Now then, leave the children to themselves to get things alone and make their crockery, get the milk from the cows, and so on. Would they be naughty then? Why, they'd die of hunger! Well, then, leave us with our passions and thoughts, without any idea of the one God, of the Creator, or without any idea of what is right, without any idea of moral evil.[4]

The "idea" here is that reality is that which God has made known to us by revelation. Any other reality is unlivable. Despite our observations of the fallen and brutal world, we are to love our neighbor as ourselves, to

4. Tolstoy, *Anna Karenina*, chap. 13.

suffer for a greater and unseen reality, because God has spoken and told us what this world actually means. Autonomous nature taught us none of this. When sinful and rebellious men are reading nature, it contradicts created order.

Unless God had presented us with a revelation of Himself, we would not know what manner of persons we ought to be. The world is intelligible because the God who spoke created it, made us able to know it, and able to know Him through it. Everything was geared for us to have communion with God. Once we are separated from God by sin, the curse of our sins presents us with a world of thorns and a ground not yielding all its possible increase. In that cursed world of sorrow, all our knowledge is skewed without God's grace. Knowing the times table, rules of logic, language, or the angles of a triangle would only be artifacts of absurdity, unable to rescue us from the skepticism of Hume or the nihilism of Nietzsche. Three times three makes nine is true enough, but so is the fact that we will suffer and die and the lion will eat the lamb alive in a traumatic manner. The angles of a triangle summing 180 degrees will, as a fact, lead us nowhere. It will not persuade the darkened mind not to strive to be the lion instead of the lamb.

Bringing this matter to our sanctification, we approach God's word ready to allow it to change how we view the world and our actions in it. The word of God ought to change our minds all the time. That is the nature of our place in the world as disciples of Christ (Matt 28:19). We walk not by sight but by faith. That is, we trust God and do what is commanded us even when it runs contrary to all else. We live in a world that we cannot fully make sense of—one in which we are made to cry out in suffering. We live in a world where we say with the psalmist to our Lord, "O send out thy light and thy truth: let them lead me" (Ps 43:3).

Take again, for instance, the observable phenomenon of self-preservation and its contradiction of the gospel. To live by sight would repudiate the words of Paul telling us that because of what Christ has done for us, we should present our bodies as living sacrifices to God (Rom 12:1). We will never arrive at that fundamental understanding of sanctification by observing or thinking about nature but by hearing the voice of God. If we are not relying on God to show us what we are to do, but instead are relying on some other form of knowing, we will never live a life of faith. We will never live for greater, unseen truths.

The news cycle does nothing but teach us to constantly hate the other. Science and philosophy that flows from sinful men constantly provide little bits of data that malign the other and cause us to think certain ways against them. Somewhere, our culture has chosen to walk only by sight without even the proverbial "leap in the dark." This expedites the darkness around us. At some point, people who name the name of Christ have come to believe that Christians should also reason in the same way. It will lead to the same bad end, for the light of the Scriptures alone can show us our paths (Ps 119:9, 128, 130). Those that ignore Scripture for little pieces of data generated by finite and fallen human minds will eventually have nothing good to say about their neighbor.

Christ prays for us to the Father as our Mediator, "Sanctify them through thy truth: thy word is truth" (John 17:17). He was not interceding to the Father for the disciples to be better logicians, better apt to observe nature and make correct conclusions from it. Rather, He posited an absolute need to hear the word of God and to be changed by it. We need to be sanctified. We need to be made holy or consecrated to God's use. We need to be like the holy vessels of the temple—washed, made clean, and set apart for God's purposes. Why did Christ pray this when He did? The context tells us that Christ was in the world with His followers and, while He was thus, He kept them. Christ was departing from them (John 17:12–13). While He was there, Christ gave them the word of God (17:14). They were being left in the world, even sent into the world as their Lord was, representing Him to this world. In this world, the evil one may overtake them (17:15–16, 18). On this ground, the disciples needed the truth of Christ to be sanctified in this evil world, a world filled with things contrary to and contradicting the gospel. The mediatorial prayer of Christ highlighted that the word of God is the means of that sanctification. To live for Christ in this world is to be fully and completely reliant on what God (emphatically "your word") has spoken.

The matter before us is the present question of how God intends to make us usable in this present world. The will of God is proved in our lives by our minds being transformed by the word. Our bodies are offered up only when our minds are captured and changed by God (Rom 12:2). This happens as we encounter the truth of God in the Scriptures, the source of sanctification.

Where does that leave the things that are vaunted up to the same level of authority as revelation—things such as human reason, empirical science, and even Christian tradition? It leaves those matters always subordinate and correctable by the word of God. It is important that we learn to reason well, but it is more important for us to submit our reasoning to what God has said. As was already pointed out, often what we reason is faulty and even contradictory to our faith. Christian history should be studied and should aid us in understanding how Christians have reasoned from the Scriptures in the past. Nevertheless, Christian history is often filled with conflict that needs to be submitted again to the Scriptures. Traditions have often arisen that contradict the clear meaning of what God has said. In those cases, the Scriptures must be allowed to correct tradition. As the disciples of Christ, we never free to refuse the One that speaks (Heb 12:25). So it is with empirical science, where what *is* tells us nothing about what *ought to be*. Studying the lilies of the field can teach you nothing meaningful unless you know the Father who so clothes you (Matt 6:28–30). The Scriptures constantly correct us as the father's voice corrects the erring child and the master's voice corrects the erring disciple.

Again, we operate and live in the realm where God has spoken. The first lie ever told was questioning that reality. Did God really speak (Gen 3:1–2)? From the beginning the tension has been and remains—will we live by truth or live by lies? Will we take and live out the doctrines given to us by God or will we depart from them? There is a fallen, brutal, hateful, irrational world we are sent into to live out the truth of God. The word of God is needed to allow us to operate for God in that world faithfully. No matter the situation, we are dealing with broken people in a broken world, and we ourselves are broken people utterly dependent on the Lord. Unless we speak about something beyond what can be seen, we can offer nothing of value to any person to whom we speak. Paul through revelation was ready to deal with the suffering of the thorn, where before it created the contradiction of strength coming out of weakness (2 Cor 12). Again, consider the words of Tolstoy's character Levin:

> Where could I have got it? By reason could I have arrived at knowing that I must love my neighbor and not oppress him? . . . Reason discovered the struggle for existence, and the law that requires us to oppress all who hinder the satisfaction of our desires. That is the deduction of reason. But loving one's neighbor reason could never discover, because it's irrational.[5]

This world is broken by sin, and it hides from God in darkness. This world in its cursed state is chaos, and light came into the world through Christ. We are lights for Christ in this dark world. We cry, "Christ or

5. Tolstoy, *Anna Karenina*, chap. 12.

chaos!" The world that hates Christ and loves its darkness, it neither comprehends the light nor loves it (John 1:1–11; 3:18–21). The word of God clothes us with Christ. We have been clothed with white raiment. We have been adorned with the truth of Christ. We are children of light and not of darkness, and we shine as lights in the world (Phil 2:15). We let our lights shine so that men may see and glorify our God (Matt 5:16). And what is that light? That light is the knowledge of God through Christ that has been made known to us in the Scriptures.

What I implore, therefore, as we take up our subject is a willingness to hear the voice of Scripture speaking. Hear the Shepherd and follow His voice in everything (John 10:27). That is what marks the sanctified Christian life. We are to embody the Scriptures in all we think and do in this world. The Scriptures adorn everything we experience or reason about in the world. We cannot just say "*Sola Scriptura*" as a doctrinal statement, but we must live it out in a sinful world that contradicts it. That is what Christ interceded with the Father for us to have. He prayed, "Sanctify them through thy truth: thy word is truth" (John 17:17).

CHAPTER 3

The True Origin Story

"In the beginning God . . ." GENESIS 1:1

"It is [God] that hath made us, and not we ourselves . . ." PSALM 100:3

WE TURN FROM METHODOLOGY to ontology. Man has a nature that defines him. The definition of man's nature is our present point of interest. Ontology deals with humanity in general. No matter the shade of skin or emerging differences between individual men, there is something that makes them commonly human. This is the sum thus far: anthropology cannot be approached as if mankind was independent from God and what God has declared to be so. Therefore, man cannot be the starting point for the study of man. If we can speak of human nature and human dignity at all, we must begin with the God that made man thus. The reason for this is clear—man is dependent, derived, contingent, and does not contain the reason for his nature in himself. Yet man in his folly believes that he can begin with himself by himself and come to know all (or at least some) truths about himself. In my previous work on sexuality, I endeavored to demonstrate the folly of such an anthropology.[1] Now I endeavor to speak in the same way on the matter of race. Man has an author and that author is God.

Man is a creature dependent on his Creator, as all other things that are created. This is even more pronounced with man, for God has declared a unique relationship of grace with man. That relationship is not revealed to exist with any other creature. Of mankind alone it is said that they are

1. Tackett, *Sex and the Gospel*, ch. 2.

created in God's image (Gen 1:26). God freely made this essential truth about man so. Man's origin, purpose, and destiny cannot be divorced from God in nature or grace. If the image of God is common to all men, it directly relates to how we see ourselves and one another. I can no more kill or slander one made in the image of God with one shade or feature as I could another. Why? That person bears the image of the God I serve and is already like me in that regard. Nor can I understand myself or the other man without that reference. At best, an autonomous study of man can declare that the other exists and behaves in such and such a way. Without God, there is only my pragmatic judgment as to whether it is advantageous for me to treat the other with cruelty or kindness. Without God, such pragmatism can bear much evil.

The origin and purpose of man metaphysically, morally, and existentially is wrapped up in his connection to God. According to the Westminster Confession, the chief end of man is to know and enjoy (i.e., delight in) God forever.[2] Since man is not responsible for his origin, he cannot define his own purpose. It is not reasonable to believe man can operate outside of the purposes and parameters set forth by his Creator. The folly of Camus and other existentialists, that to be created by God is to negate the concept of freedom,[3] is its ignoring of a greater truth—to be uncreated is for man to have no nature and no purpose. That is a high price to pay for the illusion of freedom. We depend on revelation from God to tell us who He is and who we are as dependent upon and likened to Him. We are his creatures immediately related to Him in all things.

Let us then speak of the Author of man. God is the necessary precondition for both us and our world. All that is true, good, and beautiful begins with God. He created and defined all things. As the ground of truth, we see ourselves through the Creator/creature distinction and know that He ought to be revered as the beginning of all things, including the beginning of all our knowledge. He created the world to be known, our minds to know those things, the logical structures by which we may think, and Himself as the end and goal in all that is known. As the ground of goodness, we see Him through the prism of a Lord/servant relationship. He ought to be heard and obeyed. As the ground of all beauty, we see Him through the prism of a Deity/devotee (Divine/human) relationship. He is the one we ought to seek and delight in above all.

2. The Westminster Standard, "The Standards."

3. Camus, *Myth of Sisyphus*.

If this seems like a foreign concept for anthropology or any of the sciences, especially when their starting points are developed, that is a testament to how deeply secularized we have become. The exchange of the truth of God for a lie (i.e., the worship of the creature above the Creator) has been ingrained in our fallen human culture. The noetic effects of sin, as to our thinking, must be recognized and resisted here. This, then, is the condemnation: that the light of God is known and despised (John 3:19; Rom 3:10–13).

Understanding race requires seeking God just as much as any other aspect of our nature does. Race at its starting point cannot go beyond the limit of what God has made known about man. A small variant in degree from any starting point can cause a great variance over a large space and time. One incorrect integer in a math problem can produce a wide variety of errors when working toward a resolution. This is the danger of man reasoning about man without God. Man cannot be studied as an accident of chance (i.e., naturalism), as a construct of man's own mind,[4] or as an observable phenomenon of natural law.[5] These godless starting points can and do manifest dreadful results. We know nothing about a man or a group of men when our starting point is a theoretical paradigm, a humanistic assertion, or an independent observation. What we think we know from those standpoints only becomes excuses for evil. Man is the product of the purposes of a wise and active God creating and defining man as He wills. The above false starting points are indicative of our fallen idolatrous state, suppressing the truth of God and absolutizing the creature over God (Rom 1:18–26). Sinful man would rather there be no meaning than a fearful God that knows them, knows their sin, and will bring their works into judgment. They are ready to abandon any belief in truth, goodness, or beauty if pressed toward God by them.

Even professing Christians too often embrace the false starting points above mentioned. The general dismissal of God-talk (i.e., speaking meaningfully and truthfully about God) is the folly of modernist philosophy and science. The assertion of logical positivists in the early twentieth century summed this folly up well. They taught that unless something could

4. A popular sentiment of the Left, whether in the expressive individualism of the gender identity movement or in the postmodern social construct theory of race. See chapter 8.

5. A popular sentiment of the Right arising out of a supposed position of race realism whereby it is said erroneously that nature teaches the natural inferiority of some groups. See chapter 8.

be verified through empirical means, through rigorous logical language, it could not be true. Of course, such a belief was obviously contradictory as it could not meet its own criteria for truth. Realizing the bankruptcy of this godless logic and being unable to rescue it from irrationality, these philosophical musings joined the trash heap of other failed philosophies. However, this philosophy of language, known as the verification principle, has had long-lasting effects on popular discourse. It not only invaded cosmology (being the assumption of the work of men like Einstein) but it also invaded theology. As culture moved forward, all God-talk was considered as an assertion about the way man thinks outside of verifiable knowledge. It was part of Kant's noumenal world that may be pragmatically invoked but is not knowable. In theology, God became something undefined. With the un-defining of God by consequence came also the un-defining of man. The nature of man is now thought to be putty in the mind of man to define as seems fitting. Just like God in this paradigm, man is also only a fixture of the unknowable noumenal world.

The contemporary philosophy of deconstruction does not allow for objective definition of terms—especially terms like "God," "truth," or "man." A form of faith arose that foolishly boasted itself of being beyond doctrines, formal creeds, or even objective historical claims—a kind of religious agnosticism. A new form of Christianity ceased to attempt to speak to the minds and consciences of their parishioners, calling them to faith and repentance toward God. Instead, they spoke only to undefinable feelings and emotions. This irrationality meant that nothing meaningful could ever be said about truth as well as God. What was left was a self-defeating circle, making truth claims all while being unable to speak positively about truth due to being unable to speak about God.

Those who resist defining God, however, were not entirely wrong. We cannot comprehend the greatness of God any more than a worm can comprehend human nature. We cannot start with any single point of experiential knowledge and reach God from where we are without His intervention. There is no tower of Babel that can reach unto the heavens. As has often been said, we cannot get there from here. To know anything about God, the knowledge must be revelation-dependent knowledge. Knowledge of God necessitates the self-revealing God. And God is light (1 John 1:5). All truth about God is revealed truth, and from there comes all other forms of truth. We have no other reference point by which to define Him. All we can point to is creature and not Creator. Starting with ourselves, we cannot find Him.

Some may call this the hiddenness of God, but that idea is a misnomer because reality is God declaring His glory to us. What it is, rather, is a call to humility as we admit that if we are to know anything about God or reality, we are completely dependent on Him to make Himself known. God is definable, just not by us.

God has defined Himself. The evidence is all around us. The moment we engage in coherent thought, we swim in an ocean of revealed truth. God is the epistemic ground of all things. God must exist for knowledge to even be possible. What is "the fear of God" that underpins all knowledge (Prov 1:7)? It is God made known to us. When God is revealed, it is a fearful thing. When one studies the world not wanting to see God there, they stunt their own knowledge. As C. S. Lewis pointed out, God is like the sun—we cannot look directly into Him, but without Him we cannot see anything else.[6]

By grace, we can speak meaningfully of our God, ourselves, and our world in His light. This is not only so in terms of natural revelation, but in terms of the faith that we have received from Him. Natural revelation is His truth, His goodness, and His beauty being seen as part of the furniture of reality. Special revelation regards our God, beyond His acts of creating and sustaining all things, making Himself known in history. This did not begin at Sinai, but it began at the garden. Special revelation relates man to God in a way natural revelation does not. Both are rightly called grace, for God acts freely. Special revelation, though, is grace par excellence—the infallible starting point for correctly interpreting everything. This is true in a fallen world but was also necessary for unfallen Adam. Adam learned from God directly what was true and good. Whereas some say that grace does not destroy nature, it is far more truthful to say that grace reveals, redeems, and restores nature.

Scriptures present a view of God unlike all other conceptions of deity. Unlike Eastern mysticism, it presents a Tri-personal God as the ground of all our personal and relational experience. Unlike paganism, it presents a holy and righteous God as the sole ground for morality. Unlike secular science, it presents the source of all beauty, order, and design that we experience. Scriptures intuitively speak to us about the God that we know is there, the God of truth, the Holy God of righteousness, the One expressing His goodness in His creation. He is neither a part of creation, which would

6. Lewis, *Weight of Glory and Other Addresses.*

destroy those categories, nor is He unrelated to the creation (especially man) which would make those categories unknowable.

From Genesis to Revelation, the reader is confronted with the God that they already know. This the apostle Paul pointed out to the Athenians as they ignorantly worshiped at an altar to the unknown God (Acts 17:22–31). Paul boldly declared to them that we live, move, and exist because this God is. We will be judged by this very same God. We were created by and will return to God (Eccl 12:7). We have a moral obligation to seek this God in truth. It behooves us to take care not to adopt false or fanciful views of God that are not in accordance with His revelation. In presenting these truths of God, Paul reminded these idolatrous gentiles that humanity in general is the offspring of God. All of mankind stand in relationship to God fundamentally.

The Scriptures do not attempt to rationalize the reality of God as classical arguments have done. The prophets did not approach His reality as if it depended on the strength of argumentation (i.e., our ability to posit Him as a necessary variable in an autonomous math problem). They rather challenged the mind of man with what their conscience already knows—all gods are false except the Lord who made the heavens, earth, and all things in them (Ps 96:4–5). To deny that the Lord created all is to fall into absolute vanity of thought. Contrary to secular scientific claims, the universe did not create itself and has not existed forever (either in reality or in some "imaginary" state as Hawkins posited).[7] Such absurdities violate our conscience before our God. Contrary to secular philosophical claims, like those of Kant, the independent mind of man does not construct reality.[8] "It is [God] that hath made us, and not we ourselves" (Ps 100:3).

In the context of polytheistic paganism existing at that time, which posited gods arising out of primal chaos, Moses began the words of Genesis with the phrase, "In the beginning God . . ." (Gen 1:1). The prophets did not feel the need to defend this reality. In the first verse, Moses spoke of the creation of time ("In the beginning"), the beginning of space ("the heaven"), and the beginning of matter ("and the earth"). God was already there prior to space, time, and matter.

There is no coherent theory that rescues the universe and everything in it from the status of *having been made*. Nothing in this world must be the way it is. Every value therein has the status of *having been set*. The Christian

7. Hawking, *Brief History of Time*.

8. Kant, *Critique of Pure Reason*.

message declares *the God who made them.* If someone vainly says that there is no Maker, they fluently speak absurdities. Out of nothing, nothing comes—or as the Scriptures say, "Without him was not any thing made that was made" (John 1:3). There are only two categories: *things that were made* and *the one true God that made them.* "For every house is builded by some man; but he that built all things *is* God" (Heb 3:4). Every human being shares the status of having been made and God alone has the status of Creator.

Beyond the conscience, there is the voice of revelation itself. We speak of God by grace through faith. There is a God-given simplicity in that faith. "Through faith we understand that the worlds were framed by the word of God, so that things which are seen were not made of things which do appear" (Heb 11:3). He alone is "the former of all things" (Jer 10:16; 51:19). He is before all things (Col 1:17). God alone is eternal (Deut 33:27; 2 Tim 1:17). He is "the high and lofty One that inhabits eternity" (Isa 57:15). No one that knows the God of revelation glories in man or in any other creature. We were not made by contingent things like gravity, energy, particles, or "imaginary" space and time. We were not shaped by chance. Our values were not selected blindly. We are brought forth by the purposes of the eternal God. The fool says in his heart that there is no God (Ps 14:1). All is completely reliant on Him. Nothing about us is independent of Him.

Darwin denied all purpose in nature, all *telos*. The paganism of Aristotle tried to uphold *telos* without a personal and active God, positing the idea of an indifferent unmoved mover. In that sense, there is little to distinguish Darwin from Aristotle. These are blind leaders of the blind. God actively created His purposes in all things by His wisdom and for His own glory (Rev 4:11; Eph 1:11). He is the God that created and then said that what He created was good. He delighted in the things that He made and the processes they contained.

The pagan idea of order arising from chaos, or its contemporary equivalent of random chance, is contradicted by the facts found in the world of our experience. We do not live in a chaotic world but a coherent one, a world for the knower and the things known. The heavens declare and utter speech (Ps 19:1–4). There is a language of creation that is seen in each individual living cell and a mathematical language that describes every speck of space and time. Anticipating this is the biblical description of creation as coming from the Word (John 1:1–3; Heb 11:3). Underlying everything in the universe is a command. All comes from the authority of God, as each creative day began with the phrase, "And God said . . ."

Paul said to the Athenians that God has worked in history that all nations might seek Him. All are morally responsible to seek the one true God. The idea that the nations were given over by God to serve "other gods" is not a biblical one.[9] A nation, whatever ethnicity that happens to be, is blessed to know God as their Lord (Ps 33:12). Every nation sins against God when they fail to seek Him. The absurdity of multicultural claims is that all religions proclaim different truths about the same God. Every god that is not the God of the Scriptures is a false god from which all men are responsible to repent.

God is not part of the changing universe but rather rules over all. In faithfulness to His unchanging decrees, He orders and rules it (Jas 1:17; Heb 6:16–18; 13:8). We can anchor our existence upon this solid ground. The arm of flesh fails us, and we can never step into the same river twice. God is unchanging. "For I am the Lord, I change not" (Mal 3:6). Nothing is sure without that unchanging ground. God is our North Star to navigate, our fixed constant, the reference point for all things. We joyfully sing, "Change and decay in all around I see; O Thou who changest not, abide with me."[10]

God rules over the world and the affairs of men. From paganism to postmodernism and all points in between, man is always willing to accept a god that they can manipulate and control. They can accept a god that makes no demands. The God of the Bible is the Almighty. He created all and holds all together by the word of His power (Heb 1:1–3; Col 1:16–17). He limits the proud waves of the oceans and says that they can go no further. He brings the storm and bids the storm to cease. He sends rain on the just and the unjust. He exercises complete authority in political affairs as the King of kings. The king's heart is in the hands of the Lord, and as rivers of water He turns it wherever He wills (Prov 22:1). He raises kings up and sets kings back down (Dan 4:32). He is sovereignly working in the free choices of men, even their sinful choices (Gen 50:20). He is working all things together for the good of those that love Him (Rom 8:28). It is His judgment seat that all men must face, and every knee shall bow to Him. Such a God is to be feared and held in reverence.

9. See Heiser, *Unseen Realm*.

10. Lyte, "Abide with Me."

God is righteous, pure, and holy in His very nature (Ps 22:3; Isa 6:3). He does not obey a moral law above Him, but His nature is holy and is that from which the existence of morality derives. We are presented with a God that cannot lie and a Christ that is without sin (Titus 1:2; Heb 6:18; 2 Cor 5:21). The doctrine of impeccability is that which we attach to God in general and to Christ as God in particular. "He is the Rock, his work is perfect: for all his ways are judgment: a God of truth and without iniquity, just and right is he" (Deut 32:4).

Gratefully, the Scriptures present to us God who is love and is, therefore, merciful toward us (2 John 4:8). There exists in the very nature of God a reciprocating expression of love. A unitarian or an impersonal god is not love and cannot be. Love exists because it existed in God. The Lord reveals something greater than reciprocating love existing in the blessed God. God presents us with a God that created us and loved us. Revelation is a story of Him showing His love. Therefore, we are presented with a God that is full of mercy and compassion—a God that is ready to forgive.

The sum is this: God grounds the reality of who we are, the context in which we live, and the knowledge we possess. His revelation of Himself is all our hope. What has been said is not comprehensive, but it is said in hopes of creating a starting point for our subject. We can only rightly reason when we reason from God, from what God has said about Himself, and what He has said about how all things relate to Him. We must ask, "What is man?" To answer that, we must speak of the Author of man. We are not left in the dark. The God of all truth has made Himself known to us.

CHAPTER 4

Man Related to God

"What is man, that thou art mindful of him?" PSALM 8

CERTAINTY REGARDING THE NATURE of man comes only from revelational truth. Man is not a changing or evolving reality, having become what he is now and yet becoming something else still. Man is that which God created him to be. If man was evolving, one could never say what man is. Such ideologies destroy any discussion of "human rights"—barring any certainty to what is human and what is a right. We know we are derived, contingent, and by the will of God we exist. Thus, we also know that man (any individual), or mankind (the whole of man collectively), never rises above this truth: We are what we are by the grace of God. We are not our own starting point and never arrive at being the sum of all things.

We know, moreover, that we are not insignificant. There is no such thing as an insignificant man. Evil ideologies may try to reduce certain persons to something beneath the beasts, but biblical anthropology does not and cannot do so. Our significance is something that comes to us from God as well. Our nature and reality are tied up in the nature and reality of God as Supreme. Due to our finiteness, chronologically we start from where we are, and we reach out from there. One cannot but think their own thoughts and have their own experiences. To paraphrase Calvin, we know God by knowing ourselves. Yet ontologically we begin with God. To again paraphrase Calvin, we know ourselves by knowing God.[1] Thus, anthropology begins with God.

1. Calvin, *Institutes of the Christian Religion* 1.1.47.

The proper study of man is not man. Knowing God is our only proper end. We know ourselves as we are related to God. Sinful man was first asked the question, "Where are you?" That was a question of relationship. Whatever we think we know about any given aspect of humanity (whether that be scientific, political, philosophical, personal, or relational knowledge), if that knowledge does not have a recognition and reverence of God at its foundation, then we are lost and hiding in the bushes like Adam. We may relatively know how much pressure will crush a grain of sand, but if we do not fear God then we know nothing real about the sand. Why is it here? What is its origin? What is its destiny? Studying ourselves is no different. The fear of the Lord is the beginning of all knowledge, and that includes the Platonic imperative to know ourselves. Anthropology that ignores God ends up knowing nothing distinctly about man.

Proceeding to the ontological question we ask, "What is man?" To many, this inquiry represents a crisis. It touches on the great existential questions. "Who am I? Why am I here? Where am I going?" Those questions are daunting when approaching them autonomously without God. Without God the answer is fearfully resounding: "You are nothing. You have no purpose. You are headed nowhere." People are further perplexed by the complexity of the inquiry. On one hand, we know that there is something unique and different, even noble, about humanity. There is great potential for greatness in mankind (individually and collectively). Mankind is able to send rockets to the moon and beyond. They are able to produce high culture, great works of art, and great feats of science. Humanity is capable of great acts of love in feeding the hungry and caring for the afflicted. Mankind is capable of great acts of honor, valor, and altruism. On the other hand, humanity appears to be lost, brutal, debased, debauched, dark, malicious, and evil. This is that paradox of reality we discussed in the second chapter. Humanity is an enigma.

I once read an article about the difference between apes and humans. The content itself was indefinite in its conclusions about the difference. More interesting to me at the time were the readers' comments. One reader stated that the real difference between the two was found in the fact that humans lie, cheat, gossip, kill, make war, and destroy their own environment. That comment was cynical, but it offered a good yet incomplete picture. It was accurate to our perceptions of the darkness of our nature. One cannot do a true study of man without coming to the conclusion that something is wrong. There is a reason that we lock our doors at night and that is our knowledge of other humans. As we learn from the cartoon *Scooby Doo*, the monster always ends up being a human. For all of man's potential for noble-ness, there is equal potential for evil, cruelty, selfishness, etc. Any man or woman could be a murderer, a rapist, or a child molester. The sweetest baby in the crib could grow up to be the next Hitler or Dahmer. The same hands that feed the hungry or carry the offering plate at church could be the hands that cook babies alive in microwaves. There is definitely something wrong with humanity. Yet there is dignity. We see flashing examples of those who sacrifice their lives for others and go without for the good of those that they love.

When one attempts to answer what makes us human, they can neither ignore the nobility nor the depravity. The tendency of those studying anthropology from an autonomous standpoint is to ignore one or the other of those aspects. Pascal had said that man is midway between heaven and nothing,[2] or I might say between heaven and hell. However, we prefer only one or the other of those truths. We want man to either be all noble or all dark.

Flowing from such autonomous musings are frivolous answers as to what makes man different from his closest physical simile. Materialism reduces man to a cosmic accident. Often humanity is reduced to physical traits like a larger brain, opposable thumbs, the making of tools, or the accidental alignment of chromosomes on a genetic level—all products of random changes made by a blind god called natural selection. Even the greatest minds, who start only with the assumptions of contemporary science, end up throwing their hands in the air and saying that the answer is elusive as to what makes humanity unique. Such frivolous attempts answer nothing concerning what man is. That is, they do nothing to answer the enigma, the diverse potentialities. Opposable thumbs do not tell us why we are potentially cruel or altruistic.

The same God that revealed Himself has also spoken about man. Theology and anthropology flow from revelation. There are two possibilities: man speaking of himself, or God speaking of man. There is either the voice of man speaking about himself, or there is the voice outside of man speaking about man—the finite and fallible versus the eternal and infallible. The former view of man fails. The latter is man seeing himself only as Omniscience has seen him. Sadly, man does not feel like he needs the latter. We are convinced by the closing moments of the local planetarium's

2. Pascal, *Pensées* 2:72.

presentation that we can zoom out and see the whole universe. We think that we actually figured it out by ourselves. The myth of human progress is so seductive.

The problem with man speaking about himself is that he is unable to remove himself from his own observations. Man from his autonomous view will only say what excuses himself or accuses those whom they wish to push under him. We could call this the problem of man's conscience (Rom 2:14–15). They are unable to speak objectively about themselves, or to accurately speak about others. Joseph's brothers were unable to speak peacefully to Joseph (Gen 37:4). However, God stands outside of man and is the voice of truth. This is the sure ground of anthropology.

Consider the nobility of man. David asked the question, "What is man?" The context of the question is immediately explained, and that is that God in all His greatness and glory is mindful of man.

> O Lord, our Lord, how excellent is thy name in all the earth! who hast set thy glory above the heavens. Out of the mouth of babes and sucklings hast thou ordained strength because of thine enemies, that thou mightest still the enemy and the avenger. When I consider thy heavens, the work of thy fingers, the moon and the stars, which thou hast ordained; What is man, that thou art mindful of him? and the son of man, that thou visitest him? For thou hast made him a little lower than the angels, and hast crowned him with glory and honour. Thou madest him to have dominion over the works of thy hands; thou hast put all things under his feet: All sheep and oxen, yea, and the beasts of the field; The fowl of the air, and the fish of the sea, and whatsoever passeth through the paths of the seas. O Lord our Lord, how excellent is thy name in all the earth! (Ps 8)

The text assumes the biblical truth that man has a noble and special position. That noble position is in the mind of God. There only man has his nobility. The text goes on to say that man, even though he is made in a lower status than angels (in power, in current glory, etc.),[3] is nevertheless crowned with glory and honor (that is, glory and honor above the angels). God has chosen in His mind the younger over the elder, the weaker above

3. In Ps 8, in the Masoretic Text, the text reads "made a little lower than the Elohim." This is likely due to the angels representing God in judgment, as such a title is sometimes used for men as well. The writer of Hebrews translated the term as such: "made a little lower than the angels." That translation sees the Elohim of Ps 8 as God's ministers and messengers in the invisible realm.

the strong, to make covenant sons of humanity. Man holds a certain position in the mind of God and has a status that is noble and glorified by that truth.

The psalmist puts man in a special position in creation because it places all of creation under his feet, even that of angels who are mightier. Francis Schaeffer pointed out that mankind is special because of their dual relationship.[4] Mankind has a relationship that is horizontal. Humanity is part of creation, and therefore, is related to it—part of its hierarchy. It is not particularly odd to find that man has a similar body structure to other "higher forms" of animals and is made up of the same elements as all physical creatures just on an apparent higher order. Man as such, without God, is less than vanity. He is as the grass that is perishing (Ps 62:9; 1 Pet 1:24–25). Without God, there is nothing about man that is noble, unique, valuable, or dignified above any other thing in the created order. We are dust and will return to dust. However, humanity has a vertical relationship with the Creator, which makes this dust material that is cursed to return to dust dignified. In this, man is unique above creation. Take away the vertical relationship with God, man loses all value.

Those who speak of any man or group of men as having any value or importance outside of their relationship to their God is allowing nature to destroy grace. Our thumbs, brainpans, DNA, or skin color relate us only to the creation and impart to us no nobility above the rest of creation. If there is no vertical relationship with God, there is no uniqueness to humanity. Once that vertical relationship is asserted, no man can claim any greater value than any other man. There are no altars built by monkeys; there are no places of worship for the mice. They are creatures that glorify God as creatures but are not related to God in the same way as man. In grace, God has chosen to relate to men in a way that even the angels desire to investigate (1 Pet 1:12). Man is made for a heavenly reality to know God.

Above all, the nobility of man is based on the fact that God created him in a special position in creation *as its king*. This is something done for no other reason than it pleased God to do so. Contemporary studies on humanity begin with the denial that man is a created being and then weep when they can offer no meaningful distinctions for mankind. Secularism destroys man's special place in creation. Hence, we hear pessimism about mankind, the idea that we are of no greater moral value than animals or trees. As the idea that God is dead captured the minds of mankind, so in

4. Schaeffer, *Church at the End*.

the same proportion the idea that man is dead also was proclaimed. We are reduced to purposeless cosmic accidents, no better than any other particular thing in the universe. One can easily see the devastating effect this has on categories such as morality, human dignity, liberty, etc.

Due to an irrational commitment to have only a one-dimensional relationship with all the rest of nature, without any relationship to God, humanity is reduced to being mere products of psychological or sociological forces. That is the sum and substance of the autonomous nature-versus-nurture debate. It is the folly of racial politics as well. The view of man that says the nature of any given man (in this sense his material or biological reality) determines everything about him, or at least determines his worth or virtue, reduces man to nothing more than cause and effect. There is no value or dignity in the chemical reactions in the human brain (which are deterministically ruled by nebulous natural laws). Such reactions happen commonly, everywhere. If all we are, as Dawkins taught, is organisms dancing to our DNA, then we are on par with all material reality without distinction. Some are relatively bigger and stronger than others. One can see how it allows for low thoughts of the other to be invoked—for one to call the other a parasite and nonhuman. Such dehumanizing philosophies are exactly what we are in the eyes of modern psychology or modern biology, and consequently modern race ideology (more will be said about this "realist" ideology as we progress). Ironically, those who wish to vault their race to a position of superiority by such reasoning have cut the legs out from under their arguments.

On the other end of the spectrum are those that say that man's environment, how man is nurtured by circumstances around him, is what determines all things about man (more will be said about this "constructionist" ideology as we progress). This modern sociological view reduces mankind to beings who are driven by social or environmental forces, who are products of their environment or societal structures. Once we leave the idea that man is a created being, man is insignificant, a passive and conditioned thing like all other material objects. Man is now something like Pavlov's dog responding to stimulus at best, deluded automatons at worst, tumbleweeds going wherever the winds drive them. In such a scheme, a human baby is of no more value than a dog or one's favorite electronic device. They are just programmed and conditioned things.

Neither the psychologist, the biologist, nor the sociologist can empirically ground man as noble. Where can that nobility be found? We must leave the autonomy of man and see man through the lens of theology. Otherwise, we must be willing to embrace man as valueless. The nobility of man is found in the fact that we are created, and that we are created *by God*. Further, it is not that we are just created by God, as all other things from dust particles to angelic beings are, but as has been famously said, "We are *endowed* by [our] Creator . . ." Every artist puts something of themselves into their art and so God has shown His handiwork in the things that He has made (Ps 19:1; Rom 1:18–21). When it comes to mankind, it says that in the image of God created He them (Gen 1:26–27). There is something of a self-portrait of God endowed to man that He freely gave by His grace.

There is something about humanity that is like God in a way that nothing else in creation is. This is what makes you and me unique in the created order. It is what makes it a sin and a crime to take the life of another human being. To violate the life of another human being is not just considered an act against a human being but an act against God in whose image they exist (Gen 9:6). You and I are like God or at least are representative of Him in some unique way. None of this nobility has anything to do with the things that relate us to other parts of creation. Like monkeys and bananas, we are of dust. Like the angels, we are spirits. However, we alone bear His image among them.[5] In His image is human dignity.

What then is this image or likeness of God that we bear which gives us such dignity? The image of God is the royal stamp upon man that by the authority of the Creator says to all creation, "This is the one I have chosen to rule with and represent Me to creation." It is the covenant mark of rule that makes every man (even despite their fall into sin) dignified. The word of the psalmist is that God "crowned" (*atar*) man—that is, God crowned man "with glory and honor." He royally invested man to be above all other things in the created order (Ps 8:5). This image is not a set of faculties that, to some extent, are shared by other creatures in creation, though those are communicable attributes of God given to man for him to exercise rule (intelligence, sensibility, volition, etc.). Those are incorporated in that image but are not its essence. Angels, monkeys, and dogs have varying levels of these things, some to greater or lesser levels. If there is a human being that lacks intelligence, for instance, it does not change their royal status given to them by God (or at least the remnant thereof). This is the reason that it

5. It is noted that many theologians throughout time, such as Calvin in book 1 of his *Institutes*, have made positive claims that angels are also in the image of God. This author only notes that among those theologians no positive exegetical evidence has been put forth but rather inferences from similarities of attributes or agent-related titles.

is sin to commit infanticide or to kill the infirm. The lack of will, contrary to the ethics of some who say that freedom to choose is what makes one a legitimate person, does not remove human dignity.[6] God's communicable attributes are given to aid man in their rule, and are therefore like God in His sovereignty, as an aspect of that image. Volition is needed for judgment, intelligence for weighing evidence, sensibility to incline man to mercy or severity as needed, and so on.

There are, and may be many more, intelligent beings that are not said to be in God's image. There are, and may be many more than we know, spiritual and physical beings that have emotions or sensibilities that are not in the image of God. They, like men, can show affection or avarice. If one took attributes by themselves to be the fullness of the image then it would create the possibility of there being degrees in the image, some with more and others with less of that image. Some would be more human than others because to be human is to be in the image of God. Many race-based ideologies would love to hold such an idea of the image of God. Those with less intelligence would then have less worth, and so on. To be in the image of God is to be crowned, to be recognized by God as the heir of creation. There is a sense in which that image contained righteousness, for man fell and Christ renewed that image in righteousness (Eph 4:24). However, even in their sinfulness, every human is created in the image of God. Therefore, if one could reason that they were less sinful than the other, it still would not afford them a greater sense of human dignity. Even wicked Jezebel, as the daughter of a king, was deemed worthy of dignity (2 Kgs 9:30–37). The same we may say of all men who are made in the image of God despite being sinful.

Nobility is seen in the personal act of God blessing man at his very creation. "[God] breathed into his nostrils the breath of life; and man became a living soul" (Gen 2:7). This is not the creative act given to anything else in creation other than man. The life, or breath, or spirit of man was directly given by God who is Spirit (John 4:24). The blessing of the firstborn was given to Jacob by Isaac by touch and verbal blessing. Man is more than the material realm and more than the spiritual realm. Man is spirit-quickened flesh, breathed in by God. Man sits perfectly in the middle between heaven

6. Peter Singer, a renowned atheist philosopher, famously stated that children under a certain age could be killed because of their lack of will, and self-awareness excludes them from legitimate personhood. Singer, *Rethinking Life and Death*, 181–206.

and earth, as Pascal posited.[7] Mankind is alone in being in the created world and yet having that from God which places him above it. Man has a sense of freedom that does not belong to anything else in the physical or spiritual world.[8] We may be affected by the chemical reactions in our brains, but we have some freedom to choose and act above them. Unlike the angels who are made ministers, we were given dominion.

Mankind operates in this moral reality with God-given faculties, communicable attributes of God that may be shared in greater or lesser ways with other creatures, to aid in the royal activity they do in this world. The nature of man corresponds to God and the world we are made to occupy. Man thinks, acts, and feels (i.e., possesses intelligence, volition, and sensibilities). He interacts with the world of truth, goodness, and beauty (i.e., metaphysics, ethics, and aesthetics), knowing and declaring God in his interactions. The thinking man corresponds to the truth of God. The acting man corresponds to the goodness of God. The feeling man corresponds to the beauty of God.

As an acting and choosing being, man has a higher reality that is meant to choose God for himself and for those under his reign, to delight in doing His will as free moral agents. Man can do great works. He can present himself to God, to know and do the word of God (Rom 12:1–2).

Man as a thinking being has a higher purpose to know God. God's thoughts are not our thoughts, but God has made us to come and reason *with* Him, to love Him with all our mind (Isa 1:18; Matt 22:37). We are beings that have the capacity for knowing, inquiring, seeking, and discovering. These capacities relate us and draw us to God. We are able to comprehend things in this intelligible world that God has created. We are intelligent beings engaging with the intelligibility of the created order. Man is created to know and to learn from God, and to communicate that truth to others. A lab rat may learn that this button gives food and that one causes pain, but they cannot comprehend the reason for the maze and glorify its maker.

Created in the image of God, man as a feeling being has a higher purpose to experience God, to love and delight in Him. As such, man is to delight in the work God gave them to do. Mankind is a being of deep

7. Pascal, *Pensées* 2:72.

8. It would be the author's contention that there are not actually two separate realms but one single reality of creation containing the visible and invisible things, animals and angels—but that is beyond our current topic.

feelings that often are expressed, not in words of reason, but in various forms of art. We often find that the poet can better express how we feel than the professor, the artist more than the scientist. They speak on the sublime level of our passions, the deep level of our emotional comprehension. Thus, we are able to know God emotionally, to love Him and to know His love toward us (Rom 5:5). We are a people that not only speak but also sing to and of our God.

Above all things, God has created in man a need to know and relate to God. The need to belong[9] is the ultimate existential yearning within us. We define ourselves by our relationships (I am a father, a friend, and employee of such and such). As a relational being, man is ultimately a worshiping being. There is no other terrestrial creature that builds altars of worship and prays. The angels may surround the throne of God, but they cover their eyes. We long to see our God and to approach Him. We were created to do just that, to walk with God. We are thus crowned. As such, the sum of man (regardless of ethnicity or shade of skin) is that he is an exalted being. Mankind is noble, because he is the mediator between God and creation. Man is God's steward over the world and is solely responsible for its care as the vassal of God.

God imparted to man His image—or we might even say, God imparted to creation His image in man as the one to rule over and care for it. It is there that we exist for His glory. We are in our nature the image of God and as such *we bear the image* of God. The image of God contains righteousness, as mentioned earlier. It is not meant to just describe what we are but what we do. God acted on this world and still does (John 5:17). As the images of God, we have a purpose to act in this world in accordance with God's will. The image of God is our great gift and our moral imperative to reflect God in creation. Men should see our good works and glorify God (Matt 5:16). This should touch everything in man's life and inform a real and true doctrine of work and service. That is beyond the current topic of race and must be left unaddressed.

However, we see another truth about man, which was highlighted by the writer of Hebrews when they were considering the words of the psalmist:

> What is man, that thou art mindful of him? or the son of man that thou visitest him? Thou madest him a little lower than the angels; thou crownest him with glory and honor, and didst set him

9. The human need to belong is a foundational concept of social psychology.

> over the works of thy hands: Thou hast put all things in subjection under his feet. For in that he put all in subjection under him, he left nothing that is not put under him. *But now we see not yet all things put under him.* (Heb 2:6–8)

Something is wrong with humanity. Man has not reached the height of his nobility. He has not worked righteousness. Something has hindered humanity. The writer of Hebrews clearly indicates that the hindrance related to the entrance of death (Heb 2:9). Death entered because of sin (Rom 5:12). What is man? Man is a fallen creation, a marred and corrupted image of God, crowned but unable and unfit to reign. This is not just true of some of them. All of humanity has fallen from the original exalted state.

Just as humanity cannot be understood if the image of God is denied, what we might call the *soul*, mankind cannot be understood if the reality of *sin* is denied. This is the reason why psychologists and sociologists cannot accurately predict or control human behavior. We cannot educate, change the environment, restructure entitlements, redistribute wealth, or do a thousand other political initiatives and reform man from evil. We cannot usher in heaven on earth and will always be dismayed when wickedness rises up again. We only end up with better-fed, healthier, wealthier, stronger, and better-educated murderers and thieves. "The heart is deceitful above all things, and desperately wicked: who can know it?" (Jer 17:9)

There is no logic to sin. There is no real understanding as to why man kills, rapes, and does all manner of evil. However, the fact that man does is an undeniable reality. There is no easier truth to accept than this—all have sinned. We are rarely able to give a reason for choosing those things that destroy our lives and futures for a few fleeting moments of pleasure in sin. We are sinners, what more could be said? We fell from our nobility. We are cut off from our purpose of knowing and enjoying our God and communicating that to the world. We are separated from Him in sin. We do what is wrong, even though we know it is wrong. We are guilty.

If we truly know ourselves, we will admit that in each of us lies the ability to commit the greatest of evils. We cannot say like Hazael, "But what, is thy servant a dog, that he should do this great thing?" (2 Kgs 8:13). We should rather smite our hearts and say as we see the greatest sinners, "But for the grace of God, there goes I." The denial of the existence of sin opens the door for all kinds of evil. Saying that we are sick or maladjusted instead of sinful justifies the most heinous of acts. We cannot say, in the face of the general wickedness of man, that it does not represent the truth about us, that it is just true about others unconnected to us.

To bring this back to the subject of race, here is a lesson of common sense. As one with a paler shade of skin there are certain poor urban areas that I know I cannot safely go. However, one of my darker-skinned brothers would not feel safe going to certain places either. We tend to justify our own fears while dismissing the justified fears of the other. Those are not the only dangers that common sense teaches me. I would not go to seedy motels late at night, even if they are filled with people with my shade of skin. Realists (again, a term we will deal with more fully as this topic progresses) are divorced from reality on this matter. They count the danger in one place as evidence that a certain "race" is depraved. However, they do not count it as evidence against their own "race" when similar dangers are found among those that look like them. They do not measure with the same stick for they have not engaged in honest self-assessment. In one instance they accuse, and in the other they excuse.

The fact is, there are plenty of evil representations bearing my likeness. Like Dostoevsky's character Father Zosima,[10] I believe in universal guilt. I must confess that the worse sins of others are not substantially different than sins potentially in me. The sin I see in others is my own sin. After all, are we not all transgressors of the same law and all guilty of it all (Jas 2:10)? We so readily recognize what is so familiar to our own heart but only when we see it in the other. In due course, we find a way to unjustly justify ourselves by saying, "But that is a different kind of man than myself." Like Dorian Gray, we must eventually see our own hideous self-portrait.[11]

Man is a marred image of their Creator, unfit for the dominion endowed to it, cursed from fully knowing the blessing of it, and fully unable in their God-given faculties to restore themselves from that fall. Adam was created in the image of God; he sinned and then bore children in his own sinful image (Gen 5:1). Death passed to all men (Rom 5:12). Instead of dressing the garden, they now go about in their sin to kill and destroy it. This is the tragedy of man being autonomous. If not for some common grace of God, sinful man would have already destroyed his dominion.

Man, above all else, in his sin unto death is separated from God. Adam, who walked with God, hid from God because of his guilt and fear. We do the same. Man is now dead in sins. Our sins have separated us from God

10. Dostoevsky, *Brothers Karamazov*.

11. Wilde, *Picture of Dorian Gray*.

(Isa 59:2). The works of death and philosophical excuses that men make to cover them are the symptoms of sinners hiding from God. They did not like to retain God in their knowledge (Rom 1:26).

Through death, man is also separated from his fellow man. Cain now rises against Abel. There is no way to know one another with certainty, whether another person means us good or harm. Dickens brought this matter to bear when he commented that every man is a mystery to every other man,[12] intending that we see in every man a possible danger. Man became selfish, self-centered, and covetous; he became hurtful, killed and stole to have his coveted ends. We are hurt by and we hurt others, building walls and locking doors in justified or paranoid suspicion.

Also, man became separated from himself. There is a reason why loneliness and isolation are the most common of all human experiences and the most common themes in nihilistic art. Man cannot live with other men and cannot live with himself. Because of sin, his conscience thundered against his wrongs, while his flesh ran after them. Our experience is like the town of Mansoul in Bunyan's allegory. Under the sway of Diabolus, the magistrates carried Mr. Conscience to the deepest prison in an attempt to rid the city of his judgment. Even from there, the voice of Mr. Conscience still cried out with such force that the very foundations of the city shook.[13] We may call this cognitive dissonance; what we know conflicts with what we do. As sinners we have no peace.

Further, humanity became separated from their environment. Thorns and thistles grow where man works his ground. We live long enough to know the futility of our labor, as our work is eaten up by entropy and wasted by those that follow us. Such is a major theme of despair for Solomon in Ecclesiastes. We come to know that our best state is complete vanity.

Then man became separated from all eternal hope. We know that we cannot in our natural state get to God, so there is nothing left but a fearful expectation of judgment. Man is one that knows God, knows his guilt before God, and knows that he must be judged. The doctrine of total depravity rings true. Our good works never salve our consciences enough for us to believe (and this rightly) that we can expect to close our eyes in death and be received into our God's eternal abodes. Hence, man is lost. We try to dull this knowledge with empty diversions and licentious escapes, but we always wake up with the knowledge of the wrath of God. Here is the

12. Dickens, *Tale of Two Cities*, 11.

13. Bunyan, *Holy War*.

ultimate emblem of the autonomy and independence of man, separated from the Creator forever.

Man is noble but fallen. Thankfully that is not the end of our description. What is man? Man is *redeemed and exulted.* When expounding on the truth of the Eighth Psalm, the writer of Hebrews went on to say, "[We do not yet see all things put under the feet of man], but we see Jesus, who was made a little lower than the angels for the suffering of death, crowned with glory and honor; that he by the grace of God should taste death for every man" (Heb 2:9). It is a tragedy indeed when man denies the reality of the *soul* or the reality of *sin*, but the greatest tragedy of all is that when denying these things, they also deny the reality of *salvation*. Without Jesus, man has no hope, even if he still sees the remnants of his nobility. To deny the reality of salvation is to leave man in a hopeless and meaningless state, whose only hope is to divert their thoughts from their end. Without salvation, man is left unrealized, dark, and hopeless.

The theme of redemption runs through many of man's greatest stories. There is a general recognition of its need. We fell through sin, but we (through the man Christ Jesus) now stand in righteousness. Regarding Christ we now say, "Behold the Man!" We lost the image of God's holiness and righteousness when we fell, but in Christ we have it restored unto us (Eph 2:24; Col 3:10).

Let me shortly tell you about a Man that knew no sin and yet took our death, which is the wages of our sin (2 Cor 5:21). There is a way for man to step out of darkness back into the presence of God, and back into the full dignity of his created nature. Christ is that way. It is only through the Man who is our Mediator that we are brought to God (2 Pet 3:18; John 14:6; 1 Tim 2:5). We are set with Christ in heavenly places (Eph 2:6–7). In the same text in Hebrews, we learn that:

> Forasmuch then as the children are partakers of flesh and blood, he also himself likewise took part of the same; that through death he might destroy him that had the power of death, that is, the devil. . . . Wherefore in all things it behooved him to be made like unto his brethren, that he might be a merciful and faithful high priest in things pertaining to God, to make reconciliation for the sins of the people. (Heb 2:14, 17)

We are reconciled to God through Christ. We now have peace with God (Rom 5:1). We can now have peace with ourselves, through the forgiveness of sins. We, through Christ, can begin to heal our relationships with man and even have hope for paradise. We have peace through the blood of His cross (Col 1:20). There where the first man failed (where we failed), there was a second man (God with man) that stood up for our redemption and has brought us to God. In Him we may sit down in exaltation (1 Cor 15:43–48; Rom 5:12–19; Eph 2:6).

What is man? In Christ, man is redeemed, and the soul of man is restored in nobility. He is crowned and set at the right hand of God. We leave this thought of man generally with this question: Is Christ the Redeemer of only certain "kinds" of men? Do the blessings of redemption (in their fullness) only belong to certain types of humanity? Sadly, some say that redemption is limited, that it is only for certain types of humanity. To this matter now we must speak.

CHAPTER 5

Man Related to Other Men

"And hath made of one blood all nations of men for to dwell on all the face of the earth, and hath determined the times before appointed, and the bounds of their habitation." ACTS 17:26

THE PRESENTING PROBLEM WITH anthropology is that once one claims that the study of humanity is autonomous from the revealed truth of God, then there are no concrete or objective ways to relate one man to another. Without objective truth, we are left with endless distinctions that make us differ one from another. One could never arrive at any sense of unity between people no matter how small the sample group becomes. If identical twins are compared, who share perfect parity on a genetical level, there would yet be myriads of variables that make them distinct, and therefore subjectively unequal (unequal in strength, intellect, or various other capacities). The larger sample size of a family only complicates the comparisons, and comparing different families or groups of families only does so on a larger scale. As the sample size of humanity gets bigger, the differences are compounded, and unity or equality appears to be illusive. Unless the God of the Scriptures presents man with the Creator/creature distinction, and that same God has by grace imparted to each that which gives them dignity and worth, no objective point of reference can be universally applied to all that gives true equality. All are equally created by God, all are equally ruled by God, all are equally accountable to God (though some will have more or less to account for), all equally rely upon God, and equally have only that with which God has graced them. God is the leveler of all mankind.

If it is true that every man is a mystery to every other man, we naturally in our fallen state are suspicious of one another. The less we see something like ourselves in the other, the greater the mystery or suspicion. The differences that we have are important because of our own subjective awareness of those differences. In circumstances where those differences become apparent and possibly affect my own well-being, I fear those who are obviously stronger and more agile than I am. In that fear, I would immediately begin to seek ways to level the playing ground or, better yet, to gain the advantage.

Further, the more one sees the distinctions, the more those distinctions become absolutized. The closer a man can perceive a sense of sameness in his fellow, the more that fellow becomes preferred. The further one is from that sense of sameness, the greater likelihood one is held as suspect. I tend to see an ally in the one that is like me in the same way one sees an ally on the battlefield or on the ball field with one wearing a similar uniform. That of course does not make those people truly safe to us, only less suspected by us. That "preferred" one in a different set of circumstances can easily become more suspect. After all, the most common offender is one familiar to the victim. Yet, the differences still scare us more. All manner of injustice can and does flow between men on this basis.

To some, differences or distinctions are to be dismissed as being something created by man—a social construct. This builds on Marxist conflict theory and related humanistic philosophies.[1] In the biblical sense, the differences are nonetheless "real"—even if they are not always rightly perceived. Those differences came from God who gave to every individual talent, strengths and weaknesses, shades of skin, distinct lines of lineage on the micro and macro level, and so on as it pleased Him to do. Who makes us differ from one another (1 Cor 4:7)? God makes us differ, often in very perceptible ways, and that for His own glory and not for ours. He even appears to be delighted in such differences, for He in creation seemed to be well pleased with all the vast distinctions He created (Gen 1:31). In the real terms of race, God has guided human history, created boundaries for the

1. It is true that some Christian apologists have used the language of social construction to describe the unreality of race as a true concept. However, they do not mean the same thing that a Marxist apologist means by the term (i.e., the Christian does not hold to a naturalist worldview, an ethic of equality of outcomes, a denial of original sin, societal construction of morality as destroying man's original innocence, division of mankind based on privileged and oppressed classes, etc.). It would then be unfair to lump them into this type of secular humanist thought.

nations, and in providence gave them space and time. The constructionist denies all providential work and says rather that man is a god defining himself. They claim that in the "state of nature" society was brought forth and ethical norms were created that robbed man of their freedom, constructing a reality of oppression. Race—as a kind of fall from an original egalitarian state—to them was one of the constructions used to justify oppression by those who had gained power. Man constructed race as a tool for power in such a scheme.

Constructionism weaponizes our differences. Marxism has never brought peace to its constructed classes, but rather, it's brought war and bloodshed. Grounding equality apart from God fails. As long as sinful men can perceive differences, they will use them to create hierarchies and perpetuate hatred. When man is a god constructing his own reality, it is inevitable that his reality is cruel and violent toward the other. The one deconstructing will only reconstruct another cruel reality after his imagined "just" place in it. In a fallen world, constructionism is left with people with differences involved in the struggle for survival, and in that struggle only the strong survive. If only the strong survive, what does one expect each individual or community to strive for but strength and conquest? All language that says "race" is a "social construct" (i.e., created by man) idolatrously denies that God has constructed and rules over our reality.

Just because something is false does not make its opposite true. Dismissing constructionism as false and stating rather that there are "real" differences between men sadly gives way to a different form of error. The other extreme point of the pendulum is presented to us from those who call themselves realists. These insert some form of "natural" hierarchy within humanity. Race realism is a heresy that teaches that there are some "races" that are "immutably inferior" (morally, spiritually, intellectually, etc.) "by nature" and ought, therefore, to be subservient to the superior "race." This definition is not a straw man but is drawn directly from a popular far-right advocate of this standpoint.[2] Like constructionists, these also ought to be rebuked. Ultimately, they both find themselves denying the same truth. It is God that created man and made men to differ. He did so that He might be praised and not that man might exalt himself. Both suffer from thinking of themselves more highly than they ought to think (Rom 12:3).

An inherent problem with realism is its advocates' inability to say what the "real" thing is that underpins their asserted natural hierarchies. What

2. Spangler, *Christian Race Realism.*

counts as a race? The answer is not as simple as the realist pretends. In fact, they will often not even venture to offer a clear and concise definition of race. They will just declare its reality and then begin to point out differences (e.g., the ones that are easiest to manipulate, like skin color, developed traits, and perceived cultural strengths and weaknesses, etc.). Here then we must do what we have not yet ventured to do: define the term "race."

Biblically speaking, what is race? Is it fixed and immutable (or practically so) as realism claims? Is it the three sons of Noah? If so, were they the same race while they were still alive or did that change after several generations? Certainly, the latter must be true, but where does that leave us? So much for the idea of immutability. Is it the nations listed as coming from the three sons of Noah as recorded in the Table of Nations (Gen 10)? There are around seventy different nations listed. Does that give us a fixed answer on race? The biblical terms that we most associate with race, *ethnos* or *goyim*, carry the idea of nations. However, the seventy nations never fit the rhetoric that many have with the concept of race. Realists assume, for example, that White Europeans are a single race. Nevertheless, the Table of Nations contains nothing called "European" or "White" unless you stop at the three sons of Noah, and likely not even then. The Table of Nations offers no fixed idea for race either. After the Table of Nations, other nations or peoples developed. For example, long after the Table of Nations Moab became a distinct nation, as did the Ammonites, Judah, Israel, various tribes of Ishmael, and so on. Again, if races are developed over time, as they certainly did in the biblical record, there is no immutable and unchanging thing that we can nail down with precision.

Is race the accumulation of differences in families and peoples over time due to a variety of factors? The most noticeable differences seem to consume our conversations (color of skin, body type, and cultural distinctives perceived as good or bad). Does that, however, mean that race only counts when we are able to perceive noticeable differences beyond national boundaries? Do we, like the junk race sciences of generations past, measure race by the size of the skull, the shape of the back, the length of the nose, the shade of the skin, and arbitrary ways of measuring intelligence? If so, we may end up with more races than we have nations. David may have been described as "ruddy," but that description made him unique even among his own brothers. Even so, if we make these junk sciences the definers of race, we have left the Scriptures completely. After all, the writers of the Scriptures did not even appear to care about the biological reality and counted generations by patriarchal accounting, leaving room for great amounts of genetic differences to manifest within a single nation. Even if they had known about genetics the way we speak of it today, it likely would not have mattered to them. The son of a man born from a Moabite wife was just as much a possible heir as one born by a wife of one's own tribe despite genetic differences. Regardless of possible ethnic diversity with the mother (which is decried by hard-line realists anachronistically as "race mixing"), the offspring were counted by the name of the father and not by their genetic makeup.

If perceived huge differences make races distinct from one another, at what point do smaller differences actually create new races? Setting aside that any given nation can have within its citizenship diverse individuals that have noticeable differences in appearance, measurable differences in abilities and intelligence, and so on, let me give a more absurd example. My children have noticeable differences in body type and abilities than my sister's children. Are they emerging new races of people? Maybe not! However, if after five generations those differences become more pronounced, would they become different races then? If so, why? If not, why not? Maybe it could be said that they would remain the same race because they would share the same culture and national identity. That, however, is by no means a given. Our national identity is not static. The nation we live in today might be destroyed or conquered. Even if that is not so, are we to believe that we honestly have the same cultural distinctives that our fathers and mothers five generations ago had? If so, which set of sixteen different grandparents that we call our fathers and mothers are we even talking about?

When these and hundreds of other questions about the definition of race are invoked, we do not end up with a firm immutable concept. We certainly do not end up with a biblical concept of "natural" hierarchy among men. If what someone means by the word "race" is that various families of men manifest various differences over time through a variety of factors, that is reasonable. That is something real. However, if what one means is that there are "immutable traits" that make various peoples on earth either naturally superior or inferior to other peoples, as realism claims, we have denied the biblical narrative. If such a claim is to be entertained, the claimant needs to answer the above questions with precision and define exactly what they mean by "race" or "nature." After all, realists desire to develop real and actionable politics to be practiced in the real world based on their claims. The idea that they can just say, "This is real," and never define what "this" is, is neither moral nor reasonable.

The above exercise was not intended to be sophomoric or dismissive. It was meant only to give a small sample of how difficult our topic is to define. "Race" is not easily defined even though we can say that it is not a man-made concept. It is often pointed out that "race" is not a biblical word. It is a word that we are compelled to use because of its relevance in our current culture. Some Christians argue that the term should not be used at all due to its unchristian connotations. The term is admittedly far closer to Darwinian ideology and his assertion of "favored races" through natural selection (which shares similarities with realism). Though Darwin was a supporter of abolitionism and opposed the idea of race fixity (i.e., that distinctions selected in progress became fixed features of groups of people), many disciples of Darwinism asserted that distinctions were fixed. Thus, the term "race" became a permanent concept in Western culture. Due to its relationship with Darwinian concepts, many Christian leaders eschewed the term "race" and adopted a constructionist terminology. The Christian definitely cannot use the word in Darwinian terms, but just as the terms *theos* and *logos* were used by the biblical writers to speak of God despite their cultural baggage, so we desire to speak truth to what the culture calls "race."

Hermeneutics is the practice of taking the biblical concepts and translating them into current language and culture in a meaningful way. The Scriptures in Hebrew and Greek on the micro level used words like "family" (*bayith, oikos*); on a higher level they used words like "relative" (*mowledeth, suggenes*) or "tribe" (*shebet, phulé*); and on a macro level words like "nations" (*goy, ethnos*) or "people" (*am, phulé*). There is a sense of identity one has in connection with these concepts. Scriptures speak of "my people" and "his people." None of these have a correlation to the modern concept of "race" which from its above origins focuses on genetic distinctions. It would be anachronistic to force strict genetic ideas on the biblical writers. There is, for example, only one meaningful reference to the color of one's skin in the entirety of the Scriptures: the question of whether the Ethiopian can change his skin (Jer 13:23). Skin color is a very central aspect of modern conversations of race but was incidental to the biblical writers.

Scriptural concepts then do not directly coincide with the concept of race as it is understood in our contemporary context. As has been said already, scriptural concepts do not agree with constructionist or realist definitions of race. The Scriptures offer instead a view where God is the direct Creator of man and the sovereign Lord over all emerging differences. They do not arise by chance, by nature, or by the human mind. Each human being, human family, or human collective shares unity in their nature and God's sovereign activity in their distinctives.

Darwinism cannot provide unity between men. It is committed to the belief in progress from lower to higher life forms, hierarchical concepts readily adopted by realism. This framework is antithetical to the narrative of creation. After already asserting that such progress exists, any admitted distinction begs the question as to whether that distinction makes one lower or higher in development. To say that two people are genetically similar up to 99.9 percent forces one to ask, what is contained in that 0.1 percent and how does it fit into the framework of progress? After all, it has been said that humans and chimpanzees share 98.8 percent genetic similarity (though that has lately been shown to be an inflated comparison) and that 1.2 percent difference accounts for a great deal of supposed progress. If we are morally and intellectually superior based on whatever percentage difference is present, then the same reasoning applies to all human-to-human comparisons. It is impossible in such a scheme to not give credence to some "better than" proclamations between groups. "We have this biological or cultural distinctiveness and that gives us the advantage." Once the concept of "progress" is asserted through "natural selection," semantics cannot rescue any individual or group from being defined by means of hierarchy. Given that hierarchy is asserted without scriptural warrant by realism as well, there seems to be little to differentiate it from the assertions of Darwinism.

Racial animosity arises from the failure to allow what man is revealed to be in relationship to God to define all else. Human autonomy leaves us with differences, differences that we are told make a great deal of difference in any given context, and differences that make unity impossible. As far as one is able to say, "Race is real," to that they proportionally declare one race to be "better than" another. Christian theology bears no pressure to interpret differences as differences in value. The need to interpret humanity according to the truth of God revealed then becomes apparent. It alone protects from the error of thinking we are something when we are nothing (Gal 6:3). Discussion of race, or any other distinction between people, autonomous from God, is only a recipe for division and the basest cruelty.

Unity among men is something that is given by God. Every man is a creature of God related to God as his Creator, and as such related to all other created things. Man is a wholly distinct creature separated from all other kinds of creatures. Unlike secular ideology, each individual member of mankind is in the image of God. They are not as such related to the beasts, but all animal life is placed under their feet. Leave it to the mythological stories of man to relate man to beasts (Minotaurs, Centaurs, Mermaids, etc.); it is not the biblical understanding of mankind (Ps 8). Bavinck observed:

> This origin demonstrates that the animals are much more closely related to the earth and to nature than man is. True, the animals are living beings, and as such they are distinguished from the inorganic, inanimate creatures. Hence, too, they are often called living souls (Gen. 1:20, 21, and 24). . . . Therefore the animal cannot understand man although man can understand the animal.[3]

Though lower in wisdom and strength (for now), man is also created to rule over angels (1 Cor 6:2; Rom 16:20). Again, leave it pagan mythologies to speak of the gods intermingling with men, but it is not the biblical assertion.[4] Man will be exalted to be like the angels in a specific way, in perpetual life and in not being given in marriage for the perpetuation of life (Matt 22:29–30), but they will yet be greater. Just as the devil is introduced as a beast, more subtle than any other beast, so is the whole angelic realm. Man was created to rule as the image of God over the spiritual and physical realm, the visible and invisible things of creation. Some even say this is what provoked the fall of Satan and his angels, but that is conjecture.

3. Bavinck, *Origin, Essence, and Purpose of Man.*

4. Some great theologians have taught that angels intermingled with men in Gen 6:1–4. It is, however, the contention of this author that there are other viable interpretations that maintain man's distinct nature as created in the image of God and the principle that each brings forth after its own kind. Let it be at least maintained though that God intends a greater end for man than angels. Michael Heiser, in his *Unseen Realm*, teaches that angels, like men, are created in the image of God. However, he did so with little or no support from the text and the broader context of Genesis. His argument is that when God said "let us" create man in "our" image, the plural form is God speaking to angels. This is an assumption read into the text. It ignores the lack of immediate angelic antecedents in the text, the possibility of Trinitarian understanding in line with New Testament revelation about God, the fact that the text does not result in man existing in the image of any other than God, the fact that there is a singular verb for create (the "us" acted in unity in the creation of man), and that later in the text of Genesis there is a plurality in YHWH (Gen 19:24)—which is related to early Hebraic beliefs in concepts like Two Powers. The fact that angels will one day be subject to man and have already been put under the feet of Christ by His triumph on the cross is further fodder to deny equality between men and angels.

Though abrogated by the fall (Eph 2:1–3), this is a reality that is destined to be realized through Christ who as a man made the spirits subject to Him (Col 2:15). Man does not intermingle with the beasts, or fish, or with mighty angels. Rather, man is made to be their Lord, to share humanity and a throne with Christ who is the Lord of glory.

Man is created in a special relationship (see chapter 4). Every human being shares the reality that God was mindful of them and crowned them above the rest of creation. Each human being, regardless of any distinctions that God has been pleased to give them in this world, bears the image of God before the rest of creation. Therefore, they relate to one another as one that has equal dignity and value. A king with a red robe does not differ from a king in a purple one. This is the unity given to them by God. They are all representing the noble class. Killing another man cannot go unpunished because it violates that noble nature (Gen 9:6). Let man spill the blood of animals (in wise stewardship) and let man bruise the heads of devils but let no man violate the image of God in his fellow. Outside of this truth, no negative civil liberties can be deduced.

God made all people from "one man," or of "one blood" in the Byzantine tradition (Acts 17:26). Add this to the mounting equalities—we are all equally related. If one is to use the word "race," as the French first did, to describe people who share a common lineage, here is a fundamental understanding of humanity universally. Every family today may have unique aspects of familial lineage (races at a lesser level), but ultimately, we all do indeed share a common lineage in Adam (race on the macro level). This hardly seems to be a controversial observation. If it seems outrageous to the secular mind, then it must be pointed out that any other origin story must say the same. Evolutionary biology must start with a single living cell, and after that a single pair of every other emerging form of life, from the first fish to the first humans. Such origin stories lack God to give those coincidences meaning. Only in the biblical scheme is the meaningful unity of humanity not lost. That unity persists even when we add the advent of emerging distinctions, whereas it is lost in the secular world of randomness. Biblically speaking, we are indeed a human race, even if that may at any point be divided into various familial lines.

There is unity and diversity in humanity, which is a fitting truth flowing from the Triune God. The existence of diversity does not make any better, superior, or more highly developed since that which gives each dignity and worth is found in their relationship to God. After all, that same God has said that He delights in choosing the weak, foolish, and despised things for His glory to confound the things that are considered strong, wise, or noble (1 Cor 1:26–31). The distinctions that men boast are nothing to our God who will often ennoble their opposites to overthrow them. "Let not the wise man glory in his wisdom, neither let the mighty man glory in his might, let not the rich man glory in his riches" (Jer 9:23). The distinctions themselves arise from circumstances that God brings about in order to bring His purposes to fruition. God makes one rich and another poor (Prov 22:2). God made us to differ and all we have comes from Him.

The unity of human nature makes room for the differences that exist among men. All nations (*ethnos*—the broadest level of distinctions) are from one. There are ethnicities among men. That is, there are groups of men and groups of families that in time come to share a common culture, a common language, and a common heritage in a unique way. Due to isolation, climate, and a myriad of other outward forces from God's providence, the distinctions at face value can appear profound. People can differ greatly in appearance (e.g., skin pigmentation and bone structure), speech, customs, and so on. Human dignity is not found in this things.

When men attempt to measure themselves by themselves (an unwise activity—2 Cor 10:12), differences can become arbitrarily inflated. Someone can boast that when one group's Intelligent Quotient (IQ) is compared with another group, one group is "better." The assertion that the result says something about value is the unquestioned and unwise assumption. The validity of the tool, the parity of the selection sample, and the parity of circumstances in which the tool was used are rarely brought to bear in such generalized assertions.[5] All these distinctions in themselves reflect what God is doing collectively in each group, and His reasons for isolating or enriching lie solely in the secrets of His own will (Eph 1:11). Since one does not know directly from the Scriptures why God has isolated or enriched one instead of another, there is no room to use distinctions to declare superiority in any generalized way. After all, one may be enriched in order to hasten their fall, and one may be impoverished in order to make room for greater blessing.

We will sum this up presently by pointing out that God has placed the groups in differing places. Also, God has determined different times in which they will flourish or diminish, as well as the boundaries on how

5. For example, were similarly isolated groups or groups experiencing similar generational impoverishment selected as subjects of the study?

far each can go. In this sense, race is recognized by viewing the changing borders of nations through time. "And [God] hath made of one blood all nations of men for to dwell on all the face of the earth, and hath determined the times before appointed, and the bounds of their habitation" (Acts 17:26). In other words, God actively works in all groups to determine all things about them. There is no group of people that are outside of what God is doing in history, His active working in time toward His own ends. He works in all nations commonly. God has indeed "set all the boundaries of the earth" (Ps 74:17). He will raise up Babylon to work out purposes in Israel. He will enrich Israel to punish the sins of Canaan and to enrich the world through Christ. To a greater or lesser extent, all borders have been drawn and redrawn through time, and God is the chief agent in that activity. If a nation or "race" is enriched or impoverished, it is God that brought that forth.

If what one means by "race is real" is that nations or nationalities exist, then the Christian concedes. If what is meant by "race is real" is that one of those nationalities is supreme, and that such supremacy arose because of some good thing in them that other "races" do not or could not possess, the Christian must balk.[6] Nations have emerged as history and generations have progressed. God guided the emerging of those national realities and He has told us generally what His purposes were. He made them to dwell on the face of the earth. God desired from the beginning for man to bring full dominion over the entire earth, for men to multiply and fill it (Gen 1:28). He made the world to be inhabited (Isa 45:18).

God also defines and redefines national borders so that all of them might seek Him (Acts 17:27). God creates the circumstances in the political realm that make His reality clear to all and forces the moral imperative that He ought to be sought. God makes manifest that His will and His glory is supreme. Is it not so that corrupt governance makes men long for justice and righteous governments make men rejoice with blessings? Politics tends toward the glorification of man, and their judgment demonstrates that God is the one that sets up and takes down kings (Dan 4). Blessings create a moral imperative of seeing God as their sole source (Ezek 16). The events of history work towards God's glory, for they show that man is

6. Here we may state that mores of a nation may be closer or further away from the righteous standard of God's law. Of course, one should prefer a society where murder is not praised. However, that is not a natural superiority but one that speaks of the area of faith. It also says nothing of the fallen sinfulness in all cultures. Can our nation in its corrupt state really boast of a superior morality?

reliant completely on God in every way (Acts 17:28). No nation can create its own utopia. No nation can ensure its own security (Ps 127:1—though their kings are morally responsible for doing so). No nation can sufficiently plan for all contingencies that threaten their success. All the idols that men trust and make from silver and gold are again and again in history shown to be vain (Acts 17:29).

A Christian understanding of race is God-centered. It is a belief that does not allow for any sense of superiority to emerge, moral superiority or superiority of rights. No nation is inherently inferior and meant to be subjugated (though, sin is a reproach, and God will providentially bring forth means of judgment). Evils in history have been perpetrated due to a false belief that some have a physical or divine right, a superiority, to take from others what they will.[7]

Some often mistake familiarity with rights. We might call this "circumstantial superiority." Having a generational, "blood and soil" connection to a given space gives the illusion of a superior claim to call it home over the claims of others. However, such claims cannot be generalized when it is God that draws and redraws borders in the unfolding of history. These claims are limited. I can say that my family has been in Kentucky for many generations, and I therefore have a great deal of sentimental connection to this land. Even this claim is limited, for such is only true of a small portion of my ancestors and is not even a permanent reality where the connection is legitimate. My ancestors sojourned before their arrival here. The God that brought them here can justly dispossess me of it as He did with those before my ancestors. Do the Scriptures not teach this very thing? I obviously would favor any just principles of law that would protect my relative right to stay in my home, but I recognize that God may bring forth a myriad of new circumstances that could move me and my offspring on, and allow someone else to be where I am. If God so chooses, we could again be sojourners. In fact, God was more glorified by Daniel in Babylon than Daniel at ease in Jerusalem. Our earnest prayer as a nation should be that we are righteous, and as such we please God, and from that may flow many blessings (e.g., the ability to own land and pass that real possession on to children as a heritage). Nevertheless, God has moved righteous Joseph from his home and detoured all of Jacob's children from Canaan to slavery

7. Note here that God uses such foolishness to move boundaries and often will incite nations for His glory. God has commanded wickedness to be punished on a national level by other nations. In the same way, God used wicked men to crucify Christ.

before blessing them. We cannot please God without being in His Son, and even then, we may end up as pilgrims in strange lands (Heb 11:13–16). There is nothing special about our "blood" and no inherent right we have regarding any "soil" that God cannot be pleased to take from us. If we do not have the Son, our only heritage is judgment. The earth is the Lord's and the fullness thereof—not ours (Ps 24:1). He will give it to whom He wills.

Therefore, the Christian understanding of race does not allow for racism, which is the practical separation of people into assumed natural (or constructed) hierarchies. There have been various forms of what has broadly been called "Kinism," a contemporary resurrection of tribalism. Its popular political form is found with those who oppose mass immigration and interracial marriage. For the most part one cannot assume evil intent in such beliefs. For example, my grandfather (who I in no way wish to condemn) to a certain extent would have said that interracial marriages often create cultural problems for families and children. He did not hold that interracial marriage was sinful but possibly problematic, producing problems like struggles with offspring identity. He did not hold that belief in conjunction with a belief of favored and un-favored groups. Many people in many cultures hold similar sentiments and should not be unjustly accused of racism. In the same way, popular Kinism held by political conservatives opposes mass immigration as something that lessens the probability of cultural assimilation and creates national instability. These beliefs do not fundamentally degrade the essential dignity of other groups and would not merit a charge of racism. It is only the conservative social equivalent of isolationism. The difficulty for most is to balance their personal preferences and political concerns against the light and heat that comes with changing personal and political realities. The rhetoric that defends these popular forms of Kinism often becomes indistinguishable from the rhetoric of its racist forms.

Any further mention of Kinism excludes those simpler forms. Kinism in more absolute forms does fall into sinful racial pride. It is governed by those realist ideologies we have already touched on. Sinful racial pride begins with what appears to be a benign assertion, but through sinful reasoning ends with sinful conclusions. The seemingly benign assertion of Kinism is that there is a moral obligation to "love" and therefore "prefer" one's own kin, by which they mean their own ethnicity. This rhetoric is enticing because it seems intuitive on the micro level. I love and prefer my wife over other women and my children over the children of the stranger.

We find ourselves nodding our head in agreement thus far with dangerous Kinistic beliefs. There is indeed a greater moral imperative for a man to care for the needs of his own household (1 Tim 5:8). If that is all the Kinist is saying, then most would naturally agree. How this relates to imperatives addressing our neighbor, the stranger, the sojourner, and so on is yet to be determined.[8] A lot of evil toward one's others can be snuck in under that verb, "to prefer." The idea that covenantal responsibilities toward one's family negates any concern for those outside of that covenant is outside of biblical ethics. One can have honest political conversations about the prudence of caring long-term for noncitizens, but even there it does not negate any imperative toward the stranger. It is a wicked city that will not show any care to strangers in their midst.

The problem is the seeming benignity of such an assertion. What is Kinism actually saying? "We should prefer our kin, as we prefer our own children." The claim lulls us from the fact that this is merely a premise to a greater argument. There is a conclusion in mind with these catechizing statements (see chapter 2). "I ought to prefer the people connected to my own household, *therefore* I need to apply this to broader political practice." It does not remain in the realm of personal responsibility to one's own house but forcefully invades the realm of our neighbor and renegotiates those terms. It attempts to turn one's personal fidelity into broad political action and governmental policy. Now the concept of the state is presented as the same kind of entity as the home. It is just as much an error for the Fascist to apply individual terms to the state (e.g., seeing the leader as Fuhrer or Father) as it is for the Marxist to apply "love your neighbor" to state policy. These are round pegs and square holes. There is responsibility for a nephew to care for an aunt, or a grandchild to care for their grandmother (1 Tim 5:4). However, there comes a point where that line of relationship breaks down and we are no longer talking about kin. A different set of commands and responsibilities begin to apply. At some point we cease to speak of the individual and family and speak rather of the magistrate. We do not want the magistrate acting unjustly, motivated by preference (i.e., nepotism).

If one wishes to absolutize the benign idea of familial preference, then they do so in error. They apply arbitrarily the terms "family" and "household" beyond their credible meaning. The tribes of Israel may rightly say,

8. This matter is related to the so-called principle of *ordo amoris*, which will be dealt with more particularly in chapter 10.

"What part do we have in the house of David?" Household is a limited concept that can only go so far before it begins to address something wholly different. I have a great responsibility to my immediate kin, but my great grandchildren would not have the same responsibility to their great-grandchildren. Even the doctrine of levirate marriage can only go so far in its recognition of what is and what is not kin.

The benign shifts to the malignant. They say, "We ought to prefer our own kin" (having already subtly shifted the subject from the individual to the state without notice). Then by way of a second premise they say, "Nations are (or at least ought to be) made up of kin." Kinism here offers a distinct idea for the concept of a nation and by consequence race. A nation to them becomes solely a matter of common lineage. Now every preference, care, and responsibility that belongs to my nearest kin creates a huge macro-level in-group and is called a "family."[9] It calls the soil our "fatherland"[10] and people we likely do not know a "brotherhood." They do so on the basis that we happen to have some similar physical characteristics, like skin pigmentation, and some vague connection ten to fifteen generations back to some general land more than two thousand miles away. When in most circumstances, our lineage is far more complex, superficial, and spurious than we care to admit. Often, proximity alone is the only thing that allows us to have a sense of connection with the person down the street. When we try to maintain some connection to one that looks like us who also lives a thousand miles to our west, that connection begins to diminish. They may look like us, but they no longer act like us or value the things we and our near neighbors value. We that live in the hills of eastern Kentucky are not like those who live in Seattle, regardless of similar skin pigment. There is a reason that when the Scriptures speak of empire, something that binds large areas of various communities together, something much bigger than the Greek idea of the *polis* (city-state), it describes them as beasts far different than what we find anywhere in nature (Dan 7, 8). Yet, that is the extreme application that Kinism wishes to make when applying it to modern nations.

Care for one's kin becomes the moral and political imperative for Kinism. The goal is to ensure that their "race" is kept distinct from all others.

9. I resist the urge here to correlate cultlike implications with this view of the state. Cults often adopt micro-level familial terms and apply them to mid-level group settings, and it is hard not to see this as the same activity being pressed onto the macro level.

10. The Greek term *patris* speaks of one's city of origin (Matt 13:54) and is not the same as the "blood and soil" rhetoric of Kinism.

Then comes the malignant conclusion—"Since we ought to love and prefer our own kin, and our nation is our ethnic kin, then we (as a nation) ought to prefer and only care for our own ethnicity and protect and preserve that." What is wrong with such a statement? Some would contend that there is nothing wrong with it. I appeal not to the non-Christian here. We should ask if such a publicly held belief is befitting a Christian. It is a political statement. It is a racial statement. Is it a Christian statement? There is no difference between this conclusion and David Lane's Fourteen Words (see chapter 1). Can a Christian be comfortable synthesizing Christian belief with Neo-Nazi rhetoric? In the Kinist conclusion there is no room for the stranger in our midst. Who our neighbor is now is a restricted concept where good is reserved only for some, and justice only for some. There is no place for anyone to come in or out or abide if they do not share certain relational markers (as spurious as that claim might be). There must be by the force of law bowels of mercy shut to the exile or stranger. There must be by the force of law the protection of the "race" in marriage laws, not in biblical and moral terms but in racial terms. Those not part of the protected race presently in our nation must be segregated and subjugated. As time goes on and these hard lines are allowed to fester, more harsh remedies will become necessary to separate those disparate segments from the pure "blood" and their "soil."

Every Christian heresy has its textual tradition, Kinism is no different. The huge leap from familial responsibilities to the political weal is often defended by the assertion that races or nations equal "kinds"—and each is by the creative command of God to bring forth after their own "kind" (Gen 1). However, there is no indication that diverse "kinds" of humans were made by God as with animals and plants. This may have been the initial claim of Darwin, the separate lineages that gave rise to "favored" and "less-developed" races, but it is far from biblical. "From one blood" or "one man" came the nations. Diversity of ethnicities (which is God-given) does not supersede human unity. We are all the offspring of God in that sense (Acts 17:28), the sons of Adam who is the son of God (Luke 3:38). The Hebrew word *mîn* ("kind") is a word that is never used of humanity in the Scriptures. The division of humanity into nations happened after creation was completed and after the fall. Those divisions are only described with words such as "families" and "nations," not "kinds." They carry no such commands to bring forth only after their own family or nation. White supremacist groups have favored doctrines that have insinuated various "bloodlines" arising among humanity and have tried to force them on the text of Scripture. Examples of these false doctrines include: the "mud people" doctrine,[11] the serpent seed doctrine,[12] and the doctrine of the "curse of Ham."[13] These false doctrines are ad hoc adaptations towards political conclusions. None of them would emerge from a natural reading of the Scriptures.

Another assertion is that God ordained there to be nations, and it is argued that God used men to father nations. From this they conclude that nations are families. Abraham fathered many different nations, Esau was the father of the Edomite people, and so on. There is a sense of progeny in the origins of nations. Two conclusions are reached from this argumentation. First, it is concluded that there is a one-to-one correlation between a nation and family. Some contrary points have already been argued above. In the faulty reasoning of Kinism, the command to honor one's father and mother is equivalent to a duty to honor the state. The silliness of this is apparent. Do I need to care for the state when it is old, as I would my parents? When we are told to honor the king, we must reject a false equivocation. If progeny and the state were the same, then the elderly widow across town would be just as much my responsibility or the responsibility of the state as it was her immediate grandchild. Why would Paul then need to speak of the role of the church or the responsibility of the family to care for widows at all? This faulty reasoning also destroys one's ability to differentiate between the supposed greater or lesser goods. Rahab could not be commended for acting to save her immediate household, when in so doing she denied the culture and race of her city. The Neo-Nazi rhetoric of "race traitor" would negate the good she did for her own household.

Where a nation is synonymous with progeny, the Kinist is ready to make political application. In doing so they transgress into the ordinance of the home and begin to dictate political rules for marriage, outside of those given by God. They conclude that any marriage outside of the "heritage"

11. The spurious claim of a pre-Adamite race created without the image of God; this is often connected with a "gap theory" ideology that inserts a gap of time between Gen 1:1 and 1:2.

12. The claim that Satan at the fall had sex with Eve and produced the race of Cain who was "of that wicked one" (1 John 3:12). Some also try to connect this ideology with the belief that fallen angels produced "mixed children" with the daughters of men (Gen 6:1–4).

13. The claim that due to Ham's sin against Noah (Gen 9:26–27), Ham became a cursed race of dark people.

citizenry is to the detriment of that nation. If one gives any cursory reading of Kinist argumentation related to the Scriptures and race they will discover rivers of ink spilled on this very topic. Textual arguments are usually drawn from some of the following points. In God's law given to Israel there are commandments to not take wives of certain foreign nations (Deut 7:1–6), especially for priests (Lev 21:7–9). There was a righteous enforcement of such by Nehemiah (Neh 13; Ezra 9:1–15), and there were deleterious effects of marriages outside of the commonwealth of Israel in examples like Solomon and Samson (1 Kgs 11:1–9).[14] However, these examples do not prove what the Kinist wishes to prove. Chiefly, they say nothing about the validity of an interracial marriage. The marriage commandments themselves do not bar foreign marriages categorically, and all the examples stated can easily be shown to address the concern of idolatry and not the alleged sin of "race mixing." There are many examples of marriages in old covenant Israel that benefited and blessed Israel (see Ruth). And there were permissive commands of God that allowed such foreign marriages (Deut 21:10–14).

The new covenant marks the point where the promises to Abraham go out to all nations. It contains no teaching regarding race and marriage, only the reiteration of marriage being between one man and one woman united faithfully. The only Christian injunction is the imperative to marry "in the Lord"—meaning that they are to marry based on spiritual compatibility with other disciples of Christ (1 Cor 7:39). This cannot be reduced to a physical or national concept, only the spiritual reality of fellow membership in the kingdom of Christ. We are not to be unequally yoked with (marry) unbelievers (2 Cor 6:14–16). That injunction has to do with interfaith and not interracial marriages. Certainly, it was advantageous for Abraham and Isaac to seek wives for their sons among kin who had some knowledge of the one true God, rather than wives among the daughters of surrounding idol-worshiping nations. Those things do not become an argument against interracial marriages. It is the purity of faith and not the purity of blood that was the focus.

14. Sometimes less convincing arguments such as the case law regarding the daughters Zelophehad are invoked (Num 36), which limited marriage to the tribe of the father for those individuals. Such case laws were obviously not intended to be normative for all Israel. They are rather specific to the protection of inherited land in various family lines when there is no established male heir. This was important in that agrarian society. In fact, keeping such marriages to a closely related tribe in those cases is more problematic for Kinists than it is helpful to their arguments. It says that other tribes in Israel were not considered kin.

It is worth revisiting whether or not the scriptural understanding of a nation is synonymous with common progeny as Kinism assumes—beyond the arguments already made. Of course, nations originated from a single set of brothers having the same mother and father (Ham, Shem, and Japeth). We can turn the question around. Does Kinism allow for the development of a plurality of nations out of the same progeny? Isaac produced two nations out of one womb. What made those two nations different entities? It was all the conditions, circumstances, intermarriages with other cultures, geographical isolations in time and space, and hundreds of non-progeny-related variables. For example, Edom was not just the children of Esau. Esau's move to Mount Seir created a circumstance in which the sons of Seir the Horite became intermingled with the familial and political development of Edom as a nation (see Gen 36—particularly v. 20).[15] God in His sovereign working in time made those twin brothers to differ. He brought together all the disparate variables and circumstances that caused them to develop different cultures, common laws, and common leadership that produced national identities.

This sovereign working of God caused Israel to emerge as a nation. "And thou shalt speak and say before the Lord thy God, A Syrian ready to perish was my father, and he went down into Egypt, and sojourned there with a few, and became there a nation, great, mighty, and populous" (Deut 26:5). Abraham did not continue to produce other Syrians when he was separated out by God. Nations are created by the act of God separating particular people out of other existing people. "Have I not brought up Israel out of the land of Egypt? And the Philistines from Caphtor, and the Syrians from Kir?" (Amos 9:7) Nations are not biological phenomena but providential phenomena. God raises up nations and kingdoms. As nations continue through the corridors of history, the likelihood that all citizens of that given nation share a single common ancestry becomes highly unlikely. It was not so with Israel from their beginning or throughout their history (see chapter 6).

Kinism is saying too much without having consistent biblical and logical foundations. Their spurious use of scriptural argumentation is compounded by their fixation on "natural law" (see chapter 2). Extrabiblical speculations represent much of their defense of "mono-ethnic" national

15. The Horites were related to the Canaanites (Gen 14:1–6), though not mentioned among the Table of Nations. They were mostly displaced by the children of Esau in Mount Seir (Deut 2:12–22), with the exception of Seir himself and his sons. According to the genealogical records of Esau in Gen 36, they were key to Edom's development.

identity. These arguments draw out alleged evidence for the "inferiority" of certain groups of people, making the broad application that these points flow from the "nature" of those groups. Any biblical observations are made subservient to these natural observations in their erring hermeneutic.

This is where Kinism intersects with realism. Kinists draw their understanding of "natural law" from Thomistic synthesizing of the metaphysics of Aristotle with the Christian faith. Aristotle's unmoved mover was a god that had no interest in anything outside of itself. It does not make itself known in any way. It has no presiding involvement in this world (nor can it). Such a god is wholly different from the Christian God who is active and has made Himself known in the world. Knowledge in their scheme is gained by reasoning toward God without God's aid or reasoning about things unrelated to God in themselves.[16] There is a separate place for revelational knowledge. What can be known by nature is divided from what can be known by grace in this syncretized form. This is known as the nature/grace dichotomy. To many natural law advocates, this gives rise to the belief that the Scriptures are authoritative *only* on matters of salvation, but our empirical and rational observations of the world are authoritative in all other things. "After all," they say, "we do not need the Bible to teach us how to read, do mathematics, or build rockets."

Without devolving into a polemic against natural law, a couple minimal observations are offered. First, it is correct that we do not learn three times three from the Scriptures. However, the Scriptures do give us the theistic world where three times three makes sense. It gives us revelation of a Creator who created the world and created us in His image to know and understand it. In other words, it did not arise out of chaos or chance. A knowable world comes only from the God of the Scriptures as its ground. Second, there is no point in the history of man, biblically speaking, in which man was ever without the revelational knowledge of God. Man has never been without revelation by which he could further reason about things. God was the teacher of man in the beginning. Man never independently and autonomously learned about this world. Setting all that aside, Kinism allied with realism uses natural law not to argue for a belief in three times three, but rather that there is "natural superiority" of one human group over another. They do so pretending like the Scriptures say

16. Admittedly, this of necessity is a truncated presentation of this understanding of natural law. The author only wishes to highlight the tension between this tenet of natural law and *Sola Scriptura*. For a fuller treatment of Thomistic natural law the author would recommend Johnson, *Failure of Natural Theology*.

nothing morally, metaphysically, or ontologically about themselves or their fellow human beings that can correct their alleged "natural" observations. The number of topics that they believe are covered by "natural law" observations grows and the number of topics that they believe the Scriptures can speak of is diminished. They walk by sight instead of faith, believing that they can see unaided by grace, and will not allow their sight to be corrected by faith. "We can look and see, and we can figure out all these things for ourselves." Therefore, "nature is not destroyed by grace," which to them means that grace cannot correct our view of the peoples we are talking about. "Nature, based on our autonomous observations, made those other groups inferior. These observations are completely separate from revelation and have equal authority with revelation." Natural law of this type[17] is the denial of the sufficiency of the Scriptures. For Kinism, anything about one's neighbor can be put in the circle of things we know apart from God speaking. All our anthropology and all our politics is outside of revealed truths of God, according to this error. It is what Schaffer warned us about, nature eating up grace.[18]

As an extension of "natural law" reasoning, it is asserted that a nation is that which ought to be governed by "natural affection" (the concept of *ordo amoris* will be addressed in chapter 10). There is no commandment for the magistrate to love, so they must reason outside of the Scriptures to that end. I care more about my children than I do other children. A magistrate should be concerned more about their jurisdiction than for those that are not their constituents. However, one of these is "natural affection" and the other is not. The magistrate does not act for the same reason that the grandchild does, and his responsibility does not flow from the same imperatives. They are examples derived from differing categories of morality. In a Kinistic framework, the conflating of the two is a sleight of hand. The only way to accurately translate it into public policy would be to give justice only to those who happen to look like the magistrate. The term "affection" in the natural sense invokes the idea of closeness, like parental love, which would again be inappropriately applied to politics. To assert that a supposed "Christian duty to prefer" translates into broad in-group preference dismisses basic morality and complicates the practice of justice.

17. This is opposed to a biblical belief in natural law based on God having revealed Himself in nature and that revelation being consistent with all special revelation made in history.

18. Schaeffer, *Escape from Reason*.

It encourages unequal weights and measures. It calls for a respect of persons in the exercise of judgment (Jas 2:1–10; Prov 20:10). All people know there is injustice in nepotism; how much more when it is allowed to enter the arena of politics, matters of adjudication, and economics within one's national borders. The command for the magistrate is to not be a respecter of persons (Deut 1:17).

If Kinism maintains its view of the nature of nations, then there is nothing left to differentiate it from a social Darwinist understanding of the world. The strong have a right to the weak: a right to rule them, a right to use them, a right to deny them, etc. Since this is not the stance of special revelation, and special revelation is consistent with natural revelation, then what a nation is, how a nation should rule, and how they ought to conduct themselves among other nations has a different base. Kinism turns into tribalism with all its postmodern implications—no truth (revelation), just tribal narratives. If there is no truth then there is no justice, just pre-justice (prejudice), the arbitrary preference to one's own interests. To the Kinist, biology and genetics is the narrative. It trumps all.

There is more to the idea of a nation than simple biology. Aeneas may have been the father of Romulus, but the progeny of Romulus was not a necessary component of what made Rome or a Roman citizen. One can grant that families (note the plural) help originate and reinforce nations, but one is silly to believe that the effect does not outstrip the cause. God raises nations up from forefathers (not necessarily biological fathers). Families help carry common stories, the sense of common heritage, and help facilitate the development of unifying culture. The reality of a nation does not stay strictly in that realm; it becomes something else. Israel came out of Egypt as a multitude of descendants from Jacob and a mixed multitude of others (Exod 12:38). Whoever that mixed multitude was, they integrated into the Israeli populace. Seventy souls went down into Egypt, and a great multitude came out several generations later. They all stood at the foot of Sinai, both the direct descendants and the mixed multitude, where they all received a common law and all its signs. It was that covenant of law that made Israel a nation. Constitutional or cultural unity (either strong or loose) is the necessary ingredient of a nation. There was a place for those who could not be reckoned by genealogy to enter the congregation (Neh 7:63–65).

The biblical concept of naturalization underpins the covenantal concept of nations. Examples of such include:

- Timothy, whose father was Greek, was able to receive the sign of circumcision and enter the synagogues (Acts 16:3).
- Paul could be born from Jewish parents and legitimately enjoy all the benefits of Roman citizenship (Acts 16:37).
- Ruth the Moabitess could be subject to the levirate marriage protection laws of the nation.
- Joseph could raise children with an Egyptian woman whose offspring shares in the covenant (Gen 48).
- Moses could take a Midianite wife and later an Ethiopian wife, both of which share in the commonwealth of the nation, and his children could share in the covenant (Exod 2:21, 22; 4:24–26; Num 12).[19]
- The Edomite and Egyptian could enter the land and could come into the congregation (be a full citizen) after the third and fourth generation.[20] The Ammonite and Moabite could not do so (not because of race but due to previous hostility;[21] Deut 23:1–7).
- There was room for a stranger to dwell in the gates of the families of the nation and enjoy all the protections of the law and the economy of the nation. There is no reason in Scripture to believe that this case law would not also allow for eventual naturalization as in other cases (Deut 16:11).

Whether interracial marriages are seen as advantageous in certain conditions can vary among brethren. Christians should not lord over the consciences of other believers in such matters unless specifically asked for judgment in private counsel. There is no scriptural support for the claim that such marriages disturb one's heritage, unless that marriage also causes one to turn from God to idols. The law allowed for men to take wives from

19. Note: Those that wish to deny that Moses took an Ethiopian (Black) wife, a descendant of Cush, do so by twisting the ethnic identity of the word "Cush"—which they argue to be the name of the region of the Midianites. There is no biblical citation to that end. "Cush" in the Scriptures is always a referent to Ethiopia and Num 12 is not the exception. Their arguments from the text are spurious as well. They argue that the Ethiopian wife is the Midianite wife. If that argument was true, it would not have been an issue at that point in the wilderness journey for Aaron and Miriam to complain. This is an instance of eisegesis where the natural reading is not allowed because it contradicts what one desires to believe.

20. That is, their grandchildren would be counted as natural citizens.

21. This shows wisely instructed immigration laws and prohibitions.

other nations (Deut 21:10–14). The Canaanites alone were excluded due to their idolatry and not their biology (Deut 7:1–6). The sole scriptural prohibition for any marriage is the spiritual (not physical) warning—"lest they turn your hearts to idols." Those spiritual warnings of unequal yoking to "unbelievers" are all we can truly bring to bear on the Christian conscience, much less the broader political weal.

There is an important aspect of patriarchy to marriages, families, and broader social structure. The father's name gives necessary identity to families. The blessing of fathers to children is forgotten in our culture to its detriment. However, the idea that a father can mar their heritage by giving their daughters to certain "kinds" of men outside of the spiritual context, or that their sons taking certain "kinds" of wives robs them of the blessing of that heritage, is not a biblically sound inference.

The concept of nations as kin makes for a twisted morality. Kinists repeat their catechism as if it is true: "God separated nations from one another; nations are races, and mixing races is the sin of miscegenation." This sin of "miscegenation" is not something that is clearly demonstrable in the Scriptures and is rather an imposed law based on an ill-defined concept. Fuzzy definitions produce fuzzy applications. Here I will indulge the reader with vulgar examples to show that there are no specific criteria used by the Kinists to apply their principles. Would the Kinist allow for a marriage between a light-skinned German woman and a light-skinned British man? Traditionally they would arbitrarily allow for such saying that the two are the same race (based on appearance alone), even though they do not share the same nationality (*ethnos*), culture, and so on. They have already left biblical categories in their definition of nationality. If race does not relate to the biblical term *ethnos*, what does it relate to? Britain and Germany are certainly two separate *ethnoi* in biblical reasoning. Setting aside that inconsistency, a different scenario could be set forth. Would the Kinist allow for a marriage between a darker-skinned native Hawaiian female and a lighter-skinned male from West Virginia? Such a marriage would meet the Kinist's arbitrary disapproval even though both parties share a common *ethnos*. Moving forward with fuzzy definitions, those committed to the centrality of racial identities emote their convictions irrationally and all their conclusions die the death of a thousand qualifications. Biblical moral reasoning is far more certain; it would only press the moral imperative in both circumstances that both couples serve the same Lord.

A related biblical concept of citizenship also challenges the nation-as-kin narrative. Citizenship, biblically seeking, is a covenantal reality, and outsiders were able to come into that reality. David had mighty men who were from foreign nations, such as Uriah the Hittite. Elijah was by all accounts of foreign origin and was still a prophet, a covenant prosecutor, in the nation of Israel. The idea that nations flow from a sense of "natural affection" will cause immediate contention with the idea of naturalized citizenship of foreign persons. Kinism builds an entire morality from such concepts. Their moral reasoning resembles something like this: "God created man to naturally love his own wife and children; nations arise out of this natural reality of the family, and therefore it is natural to love one's own nation (i.e., race) and prefer those over others. Since it is natural it is therefore deemed as good to prefer one's race." Such rhetoric is common. Such "natural law" reasoning operates as the equivalent of a "thus says the Lord." Any dissimilarity can be used then to downgrade access. After all, nature has set this supposed law of preference. To deny that the mechanism of the state ought to benefit the "heritage citizen" more than a naturalized one is to the Kinist the same as denying the force of gravity. One could wonder if there would be any place for a Ruth to say, "Your people will be my people." If someone like me were to begin to question this reasoning we would run the risk of being accused of denying the right of nations to "defend" themselves and "care" for their own citizens. However, the ability for one to be a citizen is the matter at question. Is the claim that to be a citizen of a nation one must have some generational connection to the land that defines the nation? Nations are, according to the Kinist, "blood and soil, people and place." In such rhetoric, no place for Uriah can exist—unless Uriah was to occupy a lower tier of access to justice than the rest. Is that the biblical teaching?

In the biblical sense, nationality flows from the normative sharing of laws, from an ultimate source of truth applying to all the people who are in a place. This is not embracing multiculturalism, an oft-repeated charge. Rather, normative law is denying multiculturalism. Truth stands as the chief variable by which people and place are defined. It says that to be a citizen one must come under the single normative principle. That is the model that God gave in making Israel a nation. Naturalizing citizens is a mono-cultural act.

One of the greatest illustrations of the naturalization of strangers is found in Moses' original instructions for the Passover. Moses stated that "there shall no stranger eat thereof" (Exod 12:43). Then Moses follows with a qualification that a servant of the household who was brought into the covenant by circumcision could eat of the Passover, while hired servants and strangers could not do so (Exod 12:44–45). This immediately removed the keeping of the Passover from being a strict biological observance. Moses also made it clear that the observance is for all who are part of the citizenry (*edah*) of Israel. "All the congregation of Israel shall keep it" (Exod 12:47). Afterwards, in general, Moses addressed the difference between the native-born person (*ezrach*—one born in the land, a natural citizen) and the stranger (*ger*—one not so naturally born into the citizenry). When a stranger was dwelling among Israel and desired to take the Passover to identify fully with the history of the citizenry, they could do so if brought into the covenant through circumcision (Exod 12:48). In other words, they could become true citizens, part of the congregation, and could thus eat the Passover. They could come under the umbrella of the common law of the nation. "One law shall be to him that is homeborn, and unto the stranger that sojourneth among you" (Exod 12:49). There is a place scripturally for one who is not biologically connected to a nation to become a full participant in its citizenry.

The demand for similarity is the demand for the impossible. It can only work in a small-scale *polis* in a limited space of time. The body politic, like the physical body of the individual, has changing aspects (blood and soil). Without an unchanging spiritual reality (i.e., law—like the soul to the body), it has no enduring identity. As space and time expand, similarities dissipate even among generational relations. Shibboleth becomes Sibboleth over time with just a few miles of separation. The "people-and-place" ideology defends the feudalistic absurdity that to be a full citizen and enjoy all its privileges one must have a generational home. That was not true in Israel, and it has not been maintained among all peoples in history. It sure is not true among much of our present citizenry.

To demand that national identity flow from natural affection asserts the naturalistic heresy that what is right is what happens to be. It also morally asserts that what I love is the way things naturally ought to be. When the Scriptures speak, they tell us that we naturally love sin and darkness (John 3:21). Could this not be moralized as well, that to do evil is natural and therefore good? Naturalism is a great support for injustice. If it is true that we naturally love and prefer our own, can that natural tendency be morally corrected by Christ (Matt 5:43–48)? Can the demand for civic virtue in any way be a correction to our natural sinfulness? The nature/grace distinction made by a form of "Christian" naturalism turns into a nature/grace separation. The oft-repeated line of the Kinist is heard ad nauseam—"Grace does not destroy nature." What they often rebelliously assert is that grace cannot correct nature at all, not even fallen nature. That clever turn of phrase is a false hermeneutic. Its transgression is its denial that God has spoken authoritatively and that what God has said defines how we interpret nature. We ought to beware of such hermeneutical commitments:

1. Assuming the Scriptures do not sufficiently ground one's understanding of a given subject (e.g., anthropology, politics, etc.).
2. Rationalizing one's chosen position by making arbitrary observations to support one's position (e.g., cherry-picked data replaces the word).[22]
3. Quoting one's favorite human authorities (instead of Scripture) to establish one's claims.

Such reasoning is a self-referencing hermeneutic built solely on human authority that cannot be corrected by the word of God and also stands in opposition to it. The issue then for this type of argumentation is whether "what is" and "what ought to be" is synonymous. An endless cycle of man speaking of his own observations of "what is" can never answer that question.

When we allow God to speak to subjects of nations, race, and this supposed "order of loves," we have a much different picture. Men do not naturally love anyone outside of themselves in a fallen reality. Man is commanded by revelational truth to love. There is no command to love only one's fellow citizens and only if they look similar. We honor our kings and obey those in authority, but there is no command to love them. Why is that? Love is immediate or should be to those with whom we have an immediate connection. We ought to love our spouse, for we are commanded to do so. The fact that without grace we struggle to do so tells us that loving someone outside of ourselves is not congruent with fallen nature. A father or mother ought to love their children. Though, they often don't. "Natural affection" breaks down after that. We can speak of brotherly love as that which ought to describe familial or spiritual kinship, but as that moves

22. For a fuller treatment of how data on race is skewed and cherry-picked, see Sowell, *Discrimination and Disparities*.

outward a new word must be used to describe our moral responsibility to love. The King James translators used the word "charity" (*agape*). The first term ("brotherly love") is immediate to a natural or spiritual kinship, and the other term ("charity") begins to apply as one moves conceptually away from those real and immediate connections.

Scripturally, "natural affection" describes who we ought to love because there is an immediate connection. Can a woman forget her nursing child (Isa 49:15)? She might do so in a fallen world, and if she does that is a violation of a natural moral imperative. To apply that to conceptual connections of fellow citizenship is to lose the force of those terms. The commandments toward natural affection are due to parentage and marriage being covenant realities directed toward those directly given to us. The Scriptures know nothing of an "order of loves," but rather commandments to love within covenantal commitments. Falling under a different moral category is a call to love one's neighbor, the stranger, and the enemy. This is against our natural inclinations.

CHAPTER 6

Israel Related to Other Nations

"What advantage then hath the Jew? or what profit is there of circumcision? Much every way: chiefly, because that unto them were committed the oracles of God." ROMANS 3:1–2

WE MUST BRING THIS matter of anthropology to a close so that we may rather swim in the deeper waters of Christology. To do so we must turn our attention to the nation of Israel, the Jewish people. Here I caution the reader with my intent. I intend now to show the sinfulness of all who are in Adam and thus the truth that all in Adam do and must die. In doing this I must highlight the sins of Israel but not of Israel alone. I must conclude that all are under sin, including the one that reads these words. Such is my conviction as drawn from scriptural truth.

Nothing has defined the discussion of race more universally than this supposedly crucial point of contention: "What about Israel?"[1] Do they hold a special place above the rest of mankind? Eschatologically, how one views the place of the Jewish people before God will define how they view their own future hope. Does Israel have a future place in God's plan? Will there be a millennial reign of Christ on this earth where all the promises to Israel are fulfilled? On the contrary, is Israel made so vile by the judgment of God that they are below the rest of humanity?

One does not spend long looking into race-based movements, whether religious or political, before Israel becomes the point of contention.

1. I say this while not discounting historical apparitions like antebellum chattel slavery, Jim Crow laws, or apartheid.

Black or White Hebrew Israelite movements seem to believe that identifying themselves as the true Israelites gives them a special advantage over the rest of mankind. Neo-Nazis and White supremacists seem content to see Jews as the scourge of humanity, something lower than rats. Whether one supports the nation of Israel by current measurements seems to be a subject of the greatest political importance. Hyperdispensationalism gives Israel a special status that ensures their future and present salvation, often regardless of their submission to Christ. Hyper-Reformed ideologies dismiss them as having no status at all.

A more basic question is, "Who was Israel?" The revelation of God is the only infallible means of answering that and myriads of other questions. Israel was a nation whose beginning was without great significance. They were just a small familial band that God chose to give grace to. Grace was not given because they were good, because they were not. It was not given because they were strong, for they were not. God by His will alone chose to draw them out of the mass of sinful nations and favor them. He brought them out of misery and slavery. He made Himself known repeatedly by the moniker, "I am the Lord God that brought you out of Egypt, out of the house of bondage" (Exod 20:2). In this sense, God says to them, "For thou *art* an holy people unto the LORD thy God: the LORD thy God hath chosen thee to be a special people unto himself, above all people that *are* upon the face of the earth" (Deut 7:6). Here then is the contention: God freely graced one people group over and instead of others. God was and is free to give mercy to whom He pleases. He chose them and blessed them. They were to be a people for Him.

> When the LORD thy God shall bring thee into the land whither thou goest to possess it, and hath cast out many nations before thee, the Hittites, and the Girgashites, and the Amorites, and the Canaanites, and the Perizzites, and the Hivites, and the Jebusites, seven nations greater and mightier than thou; And when the LORD thy God shall deliver them before thee; thou shalt smite them, *and* utterly destroy them; thou shalt make no covenant with them, nor shew mercy unto them: Neither shalt thou make marriages with them; thy daughter thou shalt not give unto his son, nor his daughter shalt thou take unto thy son. For they will turn away thy son from following me, that they may serve other gods: so will the anger of the LORD be kindled against you, and destroy thee suddenly. But thus shall ye deal with them; ye shall

> destroy their altars, and break down their images, and cut down their groves, and burn their graven images with fire. (Deut 7:1–5)

Whatever can be said about the separateness of Israel, it is God who separated them from other false gods with His intent for them to be a people devoted to the one true God alone. They were not to be unequally yoked with false worshipers. God chose Israel to drive the false gods out of the land of Canaan and establish His kingdom there. God was working in history to make Himself known by governing and leading a believing people, spiritually and militantly, against that which was opposed to Him. God loved Abraham, one that by faith believed Him (Gen 15:6), and chose to bring this nation from him (Gen 12:1–3). He used Israel, who was weak and subjugated, as He yet delights to use the weak things to bring down the strong. Was Abraham naturally good? No, he was sinful and the Scriptures bear that out. Was Jacob singularly devoted to the one true God? No, he and his house often embraced false gods. Yet, they were ultimately intended to make the one true God known in this world.

What made Israel distinct from the others? It was not their genetics. Abraham was brought out of the idolatrous people of Syria (*Aram*). "A Syrian ready to perish *was* my father, and he went down into Egypt, and sojourned there with a few, and became there a nation, great, mighty, and populous" (Deut 26:5). Not all those who had physical lineage were accounted as Abraham's true children.[2] Being genetically connected to Abraham did nothing to rescue one from a wicked estate. There remain his true children who have no genetic connection to him (i.e., Christians).[3] It was not blood that made Israel the children of Abraham and neither was it soil. God made them a nation in Egypt before He gave them a land to dwell in (Gen 46:3). The land was a land of promise, a city built by God, that they would later possess. If it was neither blood (other than the fact that they were a patriarchal tribe, for the most part) nor soil (though that would come later), what made them a nation? It was the God they received as their own and the laws that were given to them by that God that made them a people.

> Behold, I have taught you statutes and judgments, even as the LORD my God commanded me, that ye should do so in the land whither ye go to possess it. Keep therefore and do *them*; for this *is*

2. See the oft-repeated concept of the children of Belial or worthlessness (Deut 13:13).

3. See Gal 3; much like we would call Washington our forefather even if we do not know a specific genetic connection.

> your wisdom and your understanding in the sight of the nations, which shall hear all these statutes, and say, Surely this great nation *is* a wise and understanding people. For what nation *is there so* great, who *hath* God *so* nigh unto them, as the LORD our God *is* in all *things that* we call upon him *for*? And what nation *is there so* great, that hath statutes and judgments *so* righteous as all this law, which I set before you this day? (Deut 4:5–8, italics original)

Nations are nations because those nations have laws that bind their citizens together. Kinists will mock this assertion, but it is biblical. It is not asserting that a nation is an ideal reality, like a vaporous entity, but it asserts that a nation at its core is something more than the visible things we measure. Just as the body has no life without the immeasurable soul, so a nation does not exist that is not ensouled with law and a shared view of truth (that which underpins and gives continuity to shifting realities). Behind those laws are gods that possess those people. Any aspect of "blood and soil" (i.e., people and place) is meaningless if there is no binding covenant of common rule applied to all. If there was a pocket of people in our nation that repudiated our laws and operated under opposing laws, we would not consider them our compatriots. They would be "enemies domestic" (as soldiers and leaders alike are made to swear to defend against). That would be true regardless of whether they had a familial connection or a semblance of shared space. There needs to be people for there to be a nation, but that is not a static concept as assumed (as argued earlier). Patriarchy is not synonymous with genetic purity (diverse marriages happen over time). Without a binding covenant between constantly genetically changing people, there is no definite people over time. The same is true of the place. Borders may shrink or expand but without laws there is nothing that makes that space *sovereign*. All there would be is disparate individuals and families who are laws unto themselves.

Soil (in the spirit of John Frame's tri-perspective view)[4] is the situational aspect of a nation. It is circumstantial. It is the nation defined in changing historic parameters as to how far its *rule* goes. Soil is needed, but God both made Israel a nation and maintained them as a nation without sovereign soil at times. Blood is the existential aspect of the nation. People are needed for the nation to pass from one generation to another. Whereas soil deals in space, blood is an aspect of time. However, the normative aspect of a nation is its laws. The borders of the land may shrink or expand,

4. Frame, *Theology in Three Dimensions.*

the blood which operates on it may augment or remain static, but the norm must be found in a greater foundation. That allows the idea of a nation to abound further than common genetics to include others who come under that same rule. There is a place for Ruth (non-Israelite) to say that "God will be my God" and to enjoy the protections thus afforded in that covenant. There is a place for Uriah (non-Israelite) to have a home and a place among God's covenant people. There is also a place for the genetically similar to be placed outside the covenant, as it was with Esau who despised the covenant and would not be so ruled.

Once there ceases to be shared laws, there ceases to be an established people or nation. The other nations had laws, but they were laws created by men. They had gods that bound them together. All nations have gods, but blessed are the people whose God is the Lord (Ps 33:12). From these gods come laws and covenants. By "gods" here, I do not mean false gods or ideals[5] but binding ideas and presuppositions about the world from which all rule comes. Some of the laws of the nations (i.e., gentiles, non-Israelites) were just (relatively speaking) and some were not. They did reason from some knowledge of the Creator, as revealed in the light of nature and generational memory. They reasoned with a fallen nature and a fallen mind. Therefore, they could not maintain true justice. Enter then the giving of the law and the creation of the nation of Israel *as a revelation to all nations* of the rule of the one true God.

The biblical concept of a nation, and race by consequence, is far different than the Enlightenment concept of social contract theory. This theory reasons from a supposed "state of nature" to the formation of the state. Such is an unwarranted secularization of the concept of nations, producing false humanistic gods to rule over men. Social contract theory envisions a fictitious state of affairs, the "state of nature," where all men are their own gods and laws unto themselves. By their own free consent, man goes from being his own god to establishing interpersonal laws for living with other men. To paraphrase Rousseau, which sums this ideology up, man is born free and everyone is or has become bound.[6] In other words, man moves from true libertarian freedom of ruling himself to the arbitrary binding of society. This "state of nature" ideology either ends with the deification of society to bind men as it pleases (totalitarianism) or the ideological return to Eden

5. Though it is often the case that the gods of nations are made false gods, such as the secular gods that rule our nation.

6. Rousseau, *Social Contract.*

where every man is his own god (anarchy). The constant tension between those two ends is the true heritage of the Enlightenment. The social contract is a false foundation for nations, promising to rid men of a foundation built on a deity, attempting to ground nations and laws on the authority of man alone. It is, therefore, doomed to failure and inevitably produces injustice. It is historical fiction, sand for a faulty foundation. There is no "state of nature," but rather, man is created under the rule of God and responsible to seek that God in their rule.

To begin with man, as if man is a sure ground for governance, is the foolhardiness of social contract theory. What justice can be produced by the autonomous sinful man? Man is not able to rescue himself from that fallenness. The fall diminished his capacity to both naturally love his own and to care about his neighbor, his perceived enemy, and the stranger. Nations are formed as instruments of justice because man is divided not only from his immediate fellow but also all others (Gen 9:6). Where is justice to be found? Is it to be found in the conscience of man that loves to excuse themselves and accuse the other (Rom 2:15)? Justice needs revelation. Ultimately, in Israel is the revelation of the rule of God among the nations.

A "Christian" version of social contract theory and its "state of nature" is currently coming into vogue among Kinists. This touted theology states that nations arise "by nature" from the created nature of man. Therefore, man can "by reason," without special revelation, govern justly.[7] However, nations find their originating imperative to do justice from the command of God (i.e., revelation).[8] As Solomon prayed, man needs the continued

7. This is a major premise of Stephen Wolfe, a leading voice in the "Christian nationalist" movement. His premise is that nations arise from the nature of man pre-fall, from that he believes to establish the ability of man to rule by tenets of "natural law" and human reasoning. Wolfe's argumentation is spurious. He relies on a lot of counterfactual arguments such as his assertion that the entire social nature of man "would have" given rise to nations without the fall and consequently without the guidance of revelation. See Wolfe, *Case for Christian Nationalism*. The only rebuttal this author would offer here is that man is created by God to rule *with God* over the creation. Man was never created to reason and act without God's revelation. The fact that man is created with faculties in God's image to aid in rule does not mean nations flow from the nature of man without God's guidance or that nations as instruments of justice are not rather artifacts of the fall instead of the goodness of man. Unfallen man has no reason to divide and fortify against his fellow man or to punish evil acts, the things that make nations and governance necessary. If this author is also free to use counterfactual arguments, without the fall each man and his family "could have" lived directly under the authority of God made known.

8. This is true even if one rejects the idea that human government originated by the command of God to Noah (Gen 9:6). If one believes that it arises instead out of the

wisdom of God to govern (2 Chr 1:10). The existence of nations is not a grand declaration of man's autonomy but of man's utter dependence on his God. One day, the fullness of man's dominion mandate will be realized, when the kingdoms of this world will be the kingdoms of our Lord. Till then, nations are to seek God and pray "Thy kingdom come!" The concept of nations flows from the commands and providential working of God in history. We do not assert some "natural state" where we are ruling ourselves outside of the commands of God. Thus, we have the historical reality of the nation of Israel and the law that identified them.

When Cain killed Abel,[9] God would not permit men corporately to punish the sin of Cain (Gen 4:15). God appeared to rule over man directly, without the mediation of formal human government, without exercise of a rule of law by men. After the flood, God gave command for man to act as a society for the punishment of evil, which was an aspect of the Noahic covenant. Biblical history is not a "state of nature" working apart from a "state of grace."[10] Biblical history is greater than speculative history and counterfactual reasoning. There is no synthesis between the real history of God's revelation and social contract theory (or its "Christian" equivalent) that places the development of nations in the will of man unguided by God.

Philosophical musings prior to the Enlightenment focused not on the origin of nations but on their ends. The responsibility of the citizens was to participate or move toward some idea of justice or the common good. This is closer to the biblical theistic concept in the sense that it saw the role of any nation to conform to the ideal. However, without God making Himself known, men grope in darkness to feel after what that common good or just end is (Acts 17:27). The setting forth of Israel and its laws is that very revelation man needed. Nations come from God and are responsible to conform to the truth of God. Fallen reasoning cannot reach the common good, for goodness is defined by God alone. Man cannot know justice from

---

dominion mandate (Gen 1:28), it is still revelation that undergirds it. However, it does not answer questions like why Cain was not allowed by God to be judged for his murder by man.

9. This happened, obviously, when there were greater numbers of men on the earth.

10. If there was a "state of nature" at all, it ends with the judgment of the flood in the sense of man developing rule from his own will and rational nature apart from the revelation of God. Obviously, during this period there were cities built and sinful men exercising some sort of political power, but not in any sense of being able to produce justice. We can write over this time—"There was no king in those days, and men did what was right in their own eyes." This is a pattern that would later be repeated in Israel and would end in the judgment of God as the pre-flood world also did.

the sinfulness of their own fallen nature. Nothing but poison comes from a corrupt well (Jer 17:9). We rightly say then that Israel in history was God teaching man how to govern.

In real history, God commanded the exercise of human government to ensure justice on behalf of those unjustly treated. God then divided the sons of Noah up to their own inheritance. “Whoso sheddeth man’s blood, by man shall his blood be shed: for in the image of God made he man” (Gen 9:6). Governance operates as a testimony against man’s sinfulness, a testimony to man’s uniqueness in the image of God, and to God’s intent that injustice be punished. The history of nations began with a renewed dominion mandate given to mankind after man experienced the wrath of God poured out in the flood (Gen 9:1–3). God’s wrath is the ultimate backdrop of human government. Noah pronounced blessings on his three sons (Gen 9:24–27).[11] He also pronounced a curse on Canaan, the firstborn son of Ham, which was prophetic of the wrath God would later pour out against the Canaanite nations. This curse indicated that God would yet bring judgment on the sins of nations. God divided the three sons up into their own nations in the Table of Nations (Gen 10).[12] Mankind rebelled against God’s division of the nations at Babel and God scattered them in judgment in the days of Peleg into all the world (Gen 10:25; 11:1–9).

A few generations later, one of the grandsons of Eber[13] was called out of the nation of Syria to make a new nation (Gen 12:1–3). This nation would be a source of blessings to all nations. God told Abraham that in him and his seed all families of the earth would be blessed (Gen 12:3). The nations that were scattered by the will of God in judgment were to be blessed through one nation that God would raise up through one faithful man. This set the stage for God’s historical drama whereby ultimately, as Christ said, “salvation is of the Jews” (John 10:22). Abraham by faith obeying, Isaac by faith sojourning, Jacob by faith blessing became part of the narrative of faith which all who are of faith are a part (Heb 11). The children of these men went down to Egypt where God made them a great multitude of people by birth and naturalization. Then God separated them out from the Egyptians. In Egypt, they waited in chains of slavery for the promise.

Israel was destined to be given the very oracles of God, His covenants, and from them salvation would come (Rom 3:1–2; 9:1–5). This exaltation

11. In a parallel to Noah, Jacob gave blessings and curses to his sons (Gen 50).

12. This was also mimicked later by Joshua dividing the land to Israel.

13. “Eber” is where we get the word “Hebrew” (Gen 11:10–32).

was not based on racial purity. There was a prevailing sense of kinship that united them. They were the children of Israel through patriarchal accounting. That is, they were considered as true children if they had spiritual connection to the covenant (Rom 9:5–6). Racial purity is not the historical accounting of Israel. Abraham was a gentile, called out of his own country to be made a new nation. He was uncircumcised. God was able to bring a clean thing, a nation defined by the covenant relationship with God, out of the unclean. He was able to take out of the rebellious nations a particular people for Himself.

From the beginning to the end in the Scriptures, Israel was not pure in terms of Kinistic accounting. At the end of the old covenant era, under Persian rule, there were still gentiles being brought out of their nations and into the commonwealth of Israel. "And many of the people of the land became Jews; for the fear of the Jews fell upon them" (Esth 8:17). While kinship was primary, naturalization was common. Marriage outside of the tribes was also very common from the very beginning of that developing nation. The children of Joseph were part Hamitic (Gen 46:20), born of an Egyptian wife (Egypt being from Mizraim, the son Ham). This made two of the tribes (Ephraim and Manasseh) at their source genetically part Hamitic and part Semitic. Judah, the one that had the right of the firstborn, bore three surviving sons as his patriarchal line is reckoned. The oldest of the surviving sons was born from a Canaanite woman. In context, it is likely that his other two sons who were born of his daughter-in-law Tamar were also such (Gen 38).[14] Thus, the chief tribe of Israel would be a mixture of Hamitic and Semitic genetics and would also be directly related to the cursed Canaanites. We know little about from where the other ten sons of Jacob took their wives, but it is reasonable to believe that taking wives from the Canaanites was the norm. For example, at least part of the tribe of Simeon came from a marriage with a Canaanite woman (Gen 46:10). Jacob, when he took his Syrian wives (which included four children born to two different slave women—likely subjugated peoples), he promised to never cross back over that border (Gen 31:52). If any of Jacob's sons took wives and bore children, then those wives (like those of Judah, Simeon, and Joseph) were either from the Hamitic Egyptians or from the Hamitic Canaanites. At least, they did not take them from their own small familial band. Anyone that has studied the Hebrew language at any length knows that the language was heavily related to the Canaanite language and other nations

14. Tamar appeared to be taken out of the same place as Judah's Canaanite wife.

of that vicinity.[15] Such would fit with occasional pre-exodus intermarriage and trade relationships between the sons of Jacob and the Canaanites.

Nothing can be said about the nature of the marriages of Israel in Egypt prior to their enslavement, likely the same phenomenon of taking wives from other nations continued, but the nature of their slavery eventually isolated them as a people. We know that Moses took a wife, not from Israelites but from the priest of Midian.[16] Given that this marriage of Moses is more closely related to Abraham, it can be concluded that Moses later took a second wife after the giving of the law. This wife was Hamitic, of the sons of Cush (Ethiopian). When it was objected by his brethren that he took such a marriage, God Himself defended Moses (Num 12). Again, the children of Cush are the only people in the Scriptures described as having unique skin pigment. Therefore, this marriage is of particular interest to the idea of racial purity and its relationship to the law of God. It sheds light on the fact that the law itself never disallowed marriages from occurring with other "races." Examples abound including the marriage of Ruth, Rahab, the Shunamite woman that was the object of the Song of Solomon, and so on.

These points regarding genetic realities may seem menial, but they clearly demonstrate that Kinistic views of nations and races do not correspond with the biblical history of Israel (a nation directly formed by God's grace) or the law God gave them. Scriptures do not support the false concept of racial purity which is anachronistically hoisted on them by Kinists. Old Testament saints were not making marriages based on our modern understanding of genetics, and they did not have a eugenics-like goal in those marriages. Genetics is not the foundation of a nation from a biblical standpoint. Patriarchal lineage is not the same as genetic sameness. Unless one wishes to explain how racial purity can exist under the circumstances described above, the point will stand. Esther can marry a gentile king and still act as a member of her people.

Any discussion of the nature of Israel includes the place of the stranger in the assembly. The origin of Israel included a "mixed multitude" (Exod 12:38). These were not directly of Jacob but were brought out of Egypt, were part of the people who received the law from God, were a part of those who continued in the wilderness (Num 11:4),[17] and were part of those who came into the promised land. For instance, a daughter of Dan

15. Waltke and O'Connor, *Introduction to Biblical Hebrew Syntax*, 3–43.

16. A gentile, likely one of the other sons of Abraham, a son not of promise as Isaac.

17. There is a possibility in context that this is where Moses took his Ethiopian wife.

had a son of an Egyptian man. They were a part of the congregation and judged as such (Lev 24). The stranger within the gates was able to partake of the fruits of the harvest and the holy things. There was a place for them to approach the temple. The Moabite was restricted from entering the congregation (i.e., the number of the people of God—citizens) until the tenth generation. However, others could after the third generation (Deut 23:1–8). If a stranger sojourned in the land, their grandchildren could become true citizens of Israel. Setting aside the reasons for the differences in those ancient immigration laws, the point is clear that naturalization and proselytization was a reality among the people of Israel. It was codified by inspiration of God. One who was not a Jew by birth could yet be numbered among the people of Israel. The thought of Paul was not original; a Jew is one that is a Jew inwardly (Rom 2:28–29).

There were many naturalized Israelites in the old covenant. A great example is Elijah the Tishbite. What exactly is a Tishbite? It is only used regarding Elijah, and it is only speculated by some that it refers to a place called Tishbe in Gilead. However, Elijah[18] is not said to belong to any particular tribe. The adjective Tishbite (*tishbiy*) means "one who sojourns." In the first and only instance where the name is given contextual meaning, it is followed by its cognate noun *towshab*, a noun that means "a resident alien" or "sojourner." He is literally called Elijah "the sojourner from the sojourners in Gilead" (1 Kgs 17:1, author's translation). Next to Moses, Elijah is the greatest prophet in Israel's history and one indelibly connected to their eschatology, and yet he is likely not a direct biological descendant of Jacob. For a man considered so great among Israel that surviving descendants still leave an empty chair for him each Passover, this makes a powerful example of naturalization. Despite being a sojourner, he was a prophet in and of Israel. He had an official political role in their commonwealth.

Other examples of naturalized citizenship could be multiplied. While Israel dealt falsely in the days of Jacob with Shechem, there was a stated possibility that if the men of Shechem would receive the sign of circumcision, indicating that they were submitted to God as Abraham's children and servants were, they could become one people with Israel (Gen 37:15–16).[19] Later the law did limit immigration of certain people due to their

18. Elijah's name is a confession that "YHWH is my God," reminiscent of Ruth's declaration.

19. See also Gen 17:10–27—circumcision was a symbol of God's covenant with Abraham to be a God to his people.

propensity to act to the hurt of Israel and to turn the people of Israel from their God (Deut 23:3–6). Nevertheless, the same law allowed the Edomite (a fellow Semitic nation) to enter the congregation of Israel after three generations as well as the Egyptian (a Hamite; Deut 23:7–8). This case law opened up the door for the people of Israel to make judgments about future naturalizations.

David had foreign troops, possibly mercenaries. These included the Gittites who were Philistines from Gath (descendants of Egypt, the sons of Ham; 2 Sam 15:18). Among them was one named Ittai who was called a foreigner and an exile in Israel. He owned David as his king (2 Sam 15:19–21). One of the most famous of David's mighty men was Uriah (the wife of whom David committed adultery with and whom David was guilty of murdering). He was called Uriah the Hittite (2 Sam 23:39). He was a Canaanite and counted among the worthiest subjects of David. The Holy Spirit thought so well of Uriah that he was named instead of his adulterous wife in the genealogy of Christ (Matt 1:6). The Holy Spirit possibly intended by this that David's marriage to Uriah's wife was a levirate marriage, and the child that resulted from that marriage raised up the name of the dead—the name of Uriah. Such an honor was not afforded to the former husband of Ruth in that same genealogy.

Kinship was an important element to Israel as a nation, but it was not fundamental to the identity of all who were counted as its citizens. As they traversed throughout the pages of the Old Testament as a unified people, it was the law of God or the rule of God that gave them their fundamental continuity. Kinists mocking covenantal concepts as believing a "nation as an idea" do so while holding to a genetic purity fiction that ignores the greater amount of biblical data. "But he is a Jew, which is one inwardly; and circumcision is that of the heart, in the spirit, and not in the letter; whose praise is not of men, but of God" (Rom 2:29; Deut 10:16–17). In other words, it was a true covenant with God held in their heart and not symbolized by outward expressions that made one a true Israelite. If God was not their God and His law was not their delight, then no amount of biological or genetic connection could bridge that gap to make them a true Jew. In the same sense one can flaunt the laws of our nation and find themselves deprived of the rights of citizenship thereby. One can claim a biologically pure connection to Abraham and not be a true son of Abraham, but rather a child of the devil (John 8:44).

That brings us to the people of Israel in the times of Christ. Here common Jewish belief had shifted to hold to racial superiority. An attitude that being a Jew made one better, cleaner, and gave an advantage over other peoples had firmly taken root with some in that nation. They saw themselves as distinctly holding the promises of God as the seed of Abraham. "We be Abraham's seed, and were never in bondage to any man. . . . Abraham is our father. . . . We be not born of fornication; we have one Father, even God" (John 8:33, 39, 41). These are the arguments that some Jewish leaders used to reject the claims of Christ as messianic and divine. Being unmoved from this view of themselves, they in this encounter were called "children of the devil" and told that the faith that Abraham had was foreign to them. In the face of their need for Christ being declared, they picked up stones to kill Christ instead. Yet they had been warned by the very Elijah they had waited for, the forerunner of Christ (i.e., John the Baptist), that they ought not to say, "We have Abraham to our father . . . [because] God is able of these stones to raise up children unto Abraham" (Matt 3:9). That which kept them from repentance in preparation of the coming Christ and that which kept them from faith in Christ when He came was the same thing: their status as physical children of Abraham. Their fuzzy genetic status is what they believed made them the people of God distinct from all others. Paul would later say that they were ignorant of God's righteousness and went about to establish their own righteousness (Rom 10:1–4). They did not see themselves as sinners like the gentiles. They therefore saw their distinctness as that which made them righteous before God. They could be said to pray, "I am glad I am not like other men" (Luke 18:11).

The scribes and Pharisees had a missionary spirit, compassing land and sea to make proselytes, to the detriment of those converts (Matt 23:15). Being distinct from others (with distinct religious practices separating them from sinful others) gave leading Jews of Christ's day a sense of racial and cultural superiority. They held a belief that their culture was in itself salvific. This influenced a later conclusion by some in the early Jewish Christian community that in order for others to be subjects of the grace of God, they would have to adopt a Jewish identity (Acts 15). Some began to teach that becoming a Jewish proselyte was the only means of having everyday Christian fellowship. They saw those who remained uncircumcised as unclean peoples. For instance, the Jews would have no dealings with the Samaritans, seeing them as unclean (John 4). As such, when Christ spoke of the Samaritan as the one who kept the law of God by being a true neighbor to the man that fell among thieves, as opposed to the quintessential Jewish figures of the high priest or Levite who were immersed in the worship and identity of Jewishness (Luke 10:30–37), such was particularly stinging. It reminded them that a true Jew is not some outward reality. A great part of new covenant Scripture is a rebuke to such a sense of racial superiority.

The point that is of the most particular interest, and what is most heavily linked to our thesis ("In Adam all die"), is the present state of Israel. Of course, there are those who claim that those identified as Jews today have no direct connection to biblical Jews. Spurious claims are made from White and Black Hebrew Israelite groups alike that theirs is the status of true Israelites instead of the modern Israelite. Their pseudo-history finds no substantive support from secular or biblical history. They rather are claims that they use to bolster a race-based gospel foreign to the New Testament. These groups see a status as the true biological representatives of present Israel to give them a blessed advantage (much as the Jewish leaders in the time of Christ believed).

Many White supremacist groups are split on how to answer whether those that are called Jews today are indeed descendants of ancient Israel. It depends on how it best serves their present arguments. If it serves them to identify the present-day Jew with the ancient Jew (e.g., to say they are cursed in the Scriptures, called the "synagogue of Satan," and so on) then they will feel comfortable doing so. Otherwise, they are comfortable making arguments that there is no real connection between modern and ancient Jews.

The Scriptures ultimately give us a means of judging this issue. The ancient Jewish people were those who were given the law and that which was laid up in the temple as Scriptures. Christ and the apostles spoke of the Scriptures in that understood light.[20] Those Scriptures were written in the Hebrew language, copied by Jewish scribes, and passed from one generation to another. "What advantage then hath the Jew? or what profit is there of circumcision? Much every way: chiefly, because that unto them were committed the oracles of God" (Rom 3:1–2). Again, "[It is the] Israelites; to whom pertaineth the adoption, and the glory, and the covenants, and the giving of the law, and the service of God, and the promises; Whose are the fathers, and of whom as concerning the flesh Christ came" (Rom 9:4–5). The early prevailing gentile church had no indelible connection to the old covenant Scriptures as to their tedious copying from generation to generation. The early gentile church (and its many poor Jewish converts) relied

20. See Beckwith, *Old Testament Canon*.

instead on the Greek translation of the Scriptures (LXX, Septuagint) for the propagation of the gospel. Few of the early church fathers (from the second century on to the time of the Reformation) took interest in knowing the Hebrew language.[21] Lineages claimed by Black and White Hebrew Israelite groups had no known possession of Hebrew manuscripts, scribal acumen for their copying, or generational relationship to the Hebrew language. However, isolated Jewish communities in Africa, Asia, and Europe can be traced from the time of Christ, and before, and up to the time of the Reformation who did keep Hebrew manuscripts, taught the scribal language, and passed them from generation to generation.[22] It was not till the Reformation and Enlightenment that any interest was shown by the churches in Europe to know and translate the old covenant Scriptures from their original Hebrew, which required reliance on known Jewish communities to access and learn. Those Jewish communities today are the known descendants of such, genealogically connected due to social isolation through the centuries in their disparate communities "among all nations" as the Scriptures left them. This is the only sure genetic connection to that ancient people, a relationship that no one else can claim.

There is not a perfect one-to-one correlation between the people we now call Jews and the ancient twelve tribes of Israel. Like Jacob halted on his hip from his encounter with God, there is something lacking from the people of the Jews today. The twelve tribes (actually thirteen) that came out of Egypt later experienced judgment and were dispersed by being conquered by Assyria and Babylon. This became known as the diaspora. Under the Babylonian and Persian rule, the diaspora developed known and distinct communities among many different nations. At the time of Pentecost, those known communities were listed.

> And there were dwelling at Jerusalem Jews, devout men, out of every nation under heaven. Now when this was noised abroad, the multitude came together, and were confounded, because that every man heard them speak in his own language. And they were all amazed and marvelled, saying one to another, Behold, are not all these which speak Galilaeans? And how hear we every man in our own tongue, wherein we were born? Parthians, and Medes, and Elamites, and the dwellers in Mesopotamia, and in Judaea, and Cappadocia, in Pontus, and Asia, Phrygia, and Pamphylia, in

21. Origen and Jerome were a few of the known exceptions of the early fathers—the latter going to the recognized Jewish communities to learn the language.

22. Waltke and O'Connor. *Introduction to Biblical Hebrew Syntax*, 3–43.

> Egypt, and in the parts of Libya about Cyrene, and strangers of Rome, Jews and proselytes, Cretes and Arabians, we do hear them speak in our tongues the wonderful works of God. (Acts 2:5–11)

These communities represented all known remnants of the twelve tribes of Israel that remained in the diaspora after the Jews returned to Judea from the Babylonian and Assyrian captivity. There are some exceptions. For instance, Orthodox Jews did not see the Samaritans as truly of Israel due to false worship and intermarriages with gentiles, though Christ apparently counted them as among the lost sheep of the house of Israel. However, there was a recognition that all these others were true Jews who had communities distinctly dwelling among "every nation under heaven." When Rome destroyed Judea after the time of Christ, it was these existing communities of the diaspora that assimilated Jews fleeing that destruction, the communities and the descendants of which continue to this day.

There are further possible outliers in what has been called the "lost tribes of Israel," though this is not as great of a phenomenon as pseudo-historical paradigms purport. For instance, in 1 Maccabees the Jews that returned from Babylonian captivity reached out to unite in alliance with the Spartans, claiming that they were genetically related to them. The Spartans were ignorant of that claim though they were amenable to an alliance (1 Macc 12:6–18). However, contrary to claims made by certain groups, there was no recognition of a similar relationship between the ancient Israelites and any other nations in that record. Though they had dealings with nations throughout the known world at that time (e.g., African nations, Rome, etc.), they neither recognized nor attempted to create alliances based on genetic relationship with any apart from the Spartans. All such claims of relationship remain speculative only.

When the Jews returned from captivity the idea that there were any lost tribes was nearly a moot point. If one cannot speak of lost tribes at that point, then the point is moot in the inter-testamental and post-testamental periods as well. A comprehensive description of Israel was given at the end of Babylonian and Assyrian captivity in the Chronicles. There were only two of the thirteen tribes not mentioned returning from captivity to reside in Judea in Chronicles: the tribe of Dan and the tribe of Zebulun. There is a recognition that some tribes partially returned and continued to have communities in the diaspora (1 Chr 5:26). However, it appears that it was determined at that time that there were no other Israelites that could be reckoned by their genealogies (1 Chr 9:1). If there were surviving members of the tribes of Dan or Zebulun, they were so few as to likely not be mentioned in that document.

In the days after Christ, there is a tacit admission that possibly one of the tribes had perished and was no longer to be found after God's judgment. Here is halting or limping Jacob. In the Apocalypse, John gave the only list of the tribes of Israel in the New Testament.

> And I heard the number of them which were sealed: and there were sealed an hundred and forty and four thousand of all the tribes of the children of Israel. Of the tribe of Juda were sealed twelve thousand. Of the tribe of Reuben were sealed twelve thousand. Of the tribe of Gad were sealed twelve thousand. Of the tribe of Aser were sealed twelve thousand. Of the tribe of Nepthalim were sealed twelve thousand. Of the tribe of Manasses were sealed twelve thousand. Of the tribe of Simeon were sealed twelve thousand. Of the tribe of Levi were sealed twelve thousand. Of the tribe of Issachar were sealed twelve thousand. Of the tribe of Zabulon were sealed twelve thousand. Of the tribe of Joseph were sealed twelve thousand. Of the tribe of Benjamin were sealed twelve thousand. (Rev 7:4–8)

Some eschatological traditions take the seventh chapter of Revelation regarding Israel to be figurative for something other than Israel. Without taking time to defend against that view, I believe it best to take it to be an actual account of the post-Christ tribes of Israel. It appears to be a description of the promise to Abraham to become a blessing to all nations, or as Paul said about the gospel, "to the Jew first and then to the Greek" (Rom 1:16). It goes from a finite (though large) number of the tribes of Israel, and then following them is an innumerable company of people from all nations, all sharing in the promises of Christ. What is of interest in the text is what John counted as the tribes of Israel. There is only one tribe missing, which is the tribe of Dan (which matches their absence in Chronicles). It is far more likely that Dan at that point was seen to have died out under judgment or were completely assimilated into other nations as to be irreparably lost.[23]

There are other peculiarities in John's account besides the absence of the tribe of Dan which also fit a Christian understanding. There is no priesthood since Levi is named as a fellow heir among the other tribes. The preeminence of Christ is held as Judah is named first (i.e., the restored kingdom of David in Christ). The "last being first" principle holds due to

23. If there is a correlation between the twelve apostles and the twelve tribes, it could here be noted that Judas lost his place among the twelve too.

Ephraim bearing the name of his father Joseph instead of the oldest child Manasseh. These peculiarities are not enough to cause one to say this is not speaking of Israel at all. This is Israel in the eyes of the Christian who shares in the promise of Christ. It is a description of the remnant of saved Jews at that time.

The existence of physical descendants of Israelites is as true today as it was after the Babylonian captivity, in the days of Christ and Paul, and after the destruction of Jerusalem. There is Israel "according to the flesh" who without Christ has no current real connection to the former covenants. Today, they are largely those that are presently identified as Jews. A small minority of those claim a belief in Christ as their Messiah, giving them real connection to the covenants. However, the vast majority of present-day Jews reject Christ in various ways, as all other peoples do.

What place does Israel hold now? Covenant theology and dispensationalism represent two different sides of a single tension. They both attempt an answer to this one question regarding Israel as a nation: "Hath God cast away his people?" (Rom 11:1) Paul answered the tension of the question immediately by saying that God has not forsaken the Jews because Paul himself was a Jew who had received grace from God, one among many in the New Testament church (Rom 11:1–5). Does that answer the broader question? God chose to raise up a nation from Abraham, to give them laws, and to use them to bring blessings to all nations. By all appearances, they have been cast away by God. That was the central thesis of the message of Christ and His parable of the vineyard owner (Matt 21:33–44). Their God came to them in the person of the Son and they, His own people, did not receive Him. As such, the gospel went to as many as would receive Him (John 1:11–12; Matt 22:1–14). Paul described Israel as presently being a people blinded in their sins, except for there being some elect among them who have been given grace (like Paul):

> What then? Israel hath not obtained that which he seeketh for; but the election hath obtained it, and the rest were blinded. (According as it is written, God hath given them the spirit of slumber, eyes that they should not see, and ears that they should not hear;) unto this day. And David saith, Let their table be made a snare, and a trap, and a stumblingblock, and a recompence unto them: Let their eyes be darkened, that they may not see, and bow down their back alway. (Rom 11:7–10)

The divide between covenant theology and dispensationalism usually does not surround the present state of physical Israel. They agree generally that the judgment of God produced a state of blindness for Israel and as such Israel is disconnected from the promises and covenants of God. Israel was broken off as natural branches of a tree, and those who had no previous connection instead were grafted into those covenants.

It is most usually the future of Israel that is the point of contention. Dispensationalists would say that physical Israel is still God's people and therefore God will turn to Israel again. In other words, God has not cast Israel off as a whole, but things are working toward their general future salvation. The covenant theologian says that all the promises to Israel have been fulfilled in the church, made up of both Jews and gentiles. Abraham through his seed (Christ) has become a blessing to all nations. They do not look for future fulfillments for Israel building a temple, possessing land, and other such lengthy eschatological commitments.

However, the future of Israel is not of great importance to our current conversation. I hold to a covenantal view that all the promises of Abraham and Israel have been fulfilled in Christ. I do not believe there is any reason to commit to complicated plans of future events to pigeonhole promises that dispensationalists believe still stand in need of fulfillment. However, I do believe it is likely a sign of the second coming of Christ that many physical Israelites will embrace Christ. While such is not necessary to the truth of Scriptures, it seems the natural reading of certain texts. For instance, Christ said that the rejecting Israelites would not see Him again "until" they did so in faith (Luke 13:35). That word "until" could mean that unbelieving Israel will one day turn to Christ (looking on the one whom they pierced; Zech 12:10) or it could mean that some of them would indeed in the coming days look to Christ in faith in the immediate historical context. Either of these interpretations of the text are possible. Paul seemed to indicate that Israel would be grafted back into the olive tree and that event would relate to the resurrection from the dead (Rom 11:23–32).

What is important in such texts is not the future state of Israel but their present state in expectation of the second coming of Christ. Whatever one believes about the future of Israel, the Scriptures at the very least speak of the fact that physical Israel is not beyond salvation here and now. They are able now to be grafted back into the promises that they rejected in unbelief. On this, any biblical dispensationalist or covenant theologian may agree. Hyper versions of either run to hurtful extremes (e.g., Israel being beyond salvation or Israel being without need of salvation). In this stance, they stand against the vile racial ideologies of sinful men. Christ said to the leaders of this unbelieving nation:

> O Jerusalem, Jerusalem, thou that killest the prophets, and stonest them which are sent unto thee, how often would I have gathered thy children together, even as a hen gathereth her chickens under her wings, and ye would not! Behold, your house is left unto you desolate. For I say unto you, Ye shall not see me henceforth, till ye shall say, Blessed is he that cometh in the name of the Lord. (Matt 23:37–39)

Christ in the declaration of the desolation of the house of Israel did not leave them outside of possible grace. When Christ sent forth the message of the gospel after His resurrection, it was sent out starting at Jerusalem (Luke 24:47). One of John Bunyan's great books highlighted this truth, *The Jerusalem Sinner Saved*. Some of the evils of antisemitism are built on a misunderstanding of the present state of Israel. Some use the declaration of the casting-off of Israel, due to their disbelief, as a reason to wrestle against flesh and blood (Eph 6:12), against evil "Jewish" conspiracies. Suddenly their present struggle is against "racial realities" and not against spiritual realities. If the casting-off of Israel does not preclude God having grace upon Israelites, then the entirety of such a poisonous worldview is undercut.

One of the favorite epithets of race-driven ideologues against Israel is to call them demons. They will quote the words of John as if they applied to all Jews where Christ said, "I know the blasphemy of them which say they are Jews, and are not, but are the synagogue of Satan" (Rev 2:9; see also 3:9). Here the conspiracies abound and contradict. "You see, they are not really Jews." Or "You see, the Jews are really demons." All these texts say is that there were Jews who went to their synagogues who resisted and blasphemed Christ in the days of John. The history of Jewish resistance to the gospel going to the gentiles is well attested in the Acts of the Apostles. They were not real Jews in the sense that they were not true believing sons of Abraham (Gal 3:26–29). It did not keep Paul from taking the gospel to the Jews first, entering their synagogues and winning converts to Christ. It does not intend to say that every ethnic Jew can be so described. Christ as a Jewish man did not call all Jews a generation of vipers and to have the devil as their father, but He did say such of those that rejected and went about to destroy Him.[24]

24. As with any group, Jew or gentile, most are indifferent to the gospel, a few are

But let us play the devil's advocate here. Let us say that such declarations of the Scriptures did intend to say that the Jews were particularly under the sway of Satan (setting aside Christ according to the flesh, the apostles, and certain believing Jews). There is a partiality here that is not being admitted. What are all men without the seed of the woman (the Messiah)? They are the seed of the serpent (Gen 3:15). It is only grace that changes this truth. Paul stated this emphatically:

> And you hath he quickened, who were dead in trespasses and sins; Wherein in time past ye walked according to the course of this world, according to the prince of the power of the air, the spirit that now worketh in the children of disobedience: Among whom also we all had our conversation in times past in the lusts of our flesh, fulfilling the desires of the flesh and of the mind; and were by nature the children of wrath, even as others. (Eph 2:1–3)

Committing to a view that the cursed language applies to unbelieving Jews literally but has no application to my own racial reality is unbiblical. "Cursed" is "everyone" not continuing in all things written in the law (Gal 3:10). We are all children under the influence of the devil and deserving of the wrath of God. Only the gospel of Christ and the grace that flows from that can change these truths about us and about them.

One text that antisemitic groups tout is:

> For ye, brethren, became followers of the churches of God which in Judaea are in Christ Jesus: for ye also have suffered like things of your own countrymen, even as they have of the Jews: Who both killed the Lord Jesus, and their own prophets, and have persecuted us; and they please not God, and are contrary to all men: Forbidding us to speak to the Gentiles that they might be saved, to fill up their sins alway: for the wrath is come upon them to the uttermost. (1 Thess 2:14–16)

Here are the same unequal scales being applied. The Jewish resistance was just like the gentile resistance. There is no reason to see one national resistance being of greater evil than the other. Further, there is no reason to see the judgment as going beyond the specific actors Paul spoke about.

Here then is the truth of the present blindness of Israel. All the advantages that they were favored with under the old covenant are now moot. It is not that we should cease to speak of the Jews as a people with dignity

---

vocally against it, and some are receptive to it. That has been the experience of this author in evangelistic outreach.

in the image of God just as we all are. It is not that we should cease to speak of Israel as a national reality with rights and able to do either good or evil, and to be judged as such. What we can no longer do scripturally is see them as "favored" or "having an advantage" spiritually over other men. The casting-off of Israel brought them down to the same level as all other peoples. It did not make them lower than other peoples. It did not make them more wicked than other peoples. The scriptural language that is used is this: "There is now no difference." Peter, when defending the gospel going out to the gentile (non-Israelite) nations without deference to Jewish proselytizing, stated that "[God] put no difference between us [Jews] and them" when He gave the gentiles faith (Acts 15:9). God did not judge these different peoples differently. Paul followed suit in his Letter to the Romans, stating that all are sinners and all may call on God in faith (Rom 3:22; 10:12). Contrary to what vile racial theorists say, as Peter pointed out when he as a Jew preached the gospel to other nations, "Of a truth I perceive that God is no respecter of persons: But in every nation he that feareth him, and worketh righteousness, is accepted with him" (Acts 10:34–35). Current hatred of Jews and embracing of supremacist ideologies turn this truth on its head. Current ideologies that make Jews "particularly pernicious among men" are fancies of depraved minds seeking reasons to hate and destroy others while exalting themselves.

The truth underlying the book of Hosea is a good object lesson to bring this out. There Hosea makes a prophecy regarding the declaration to Israel that they will be rejected but will yet be subjects of grace. There would be a time that it would be said to them that they are no longer God's people. Then Hosea went on to say, "And it shall come to pass, that in the place where it was said unto them, Ye are not my people, there it shall be said unto them, Ye are the sons of the living God" (Hos 1:10). Here we see the nature of the casting-off. They ceased to be the people of God. What does that make them? It makes them the same as all other races of men, including ours. There is an expansion of the grace promised, however. When Paul quoted the promise of gathering many sons of God in Hosea, it was understood that it would include Jews and gentiles (Rom 9:23–26). Peter included in that promise all that would be built on Christ (1 Pet 2). As Paul said, "For God hath concluded them all in unbelief, that he might have mercy upon all" (Rom 11:32).

This then is the sum of this line of thought. Israel has been reduced to the state of unbelief like all other people. There is an equal sense of doom that is over all people separated from God in this world. All are under sin. As Paul said to the philosophers at Mars Hill, "[God has commanded] all men everywhere to repent: Because he hath appointed a day, in the which he will judge the world in righteousness by that man whom he hath ordained; whereof he hath given assurance unto all men, in that he hath raised him from the dead" (Acts 17:30–31). Whatever can be said in the vilest terms about Jews, their sinfulness and opposition to Christ, can be said as well to all races of men. There is a judgment coming and all nations of men are on the wrong side of that judgment, both Jew and gentile. "In Adam all die."

PART 2

In Christ All Shall Be Made Alive

INTRODUCTION

THERE IS A COMMON truth that belongs to all men as created in God's image and bearing that image in this world. There is not a varying degree of this image in men. All who are of Adam were created to be crowned over the rest of God's creation. That image, though tarnished by sin, remains as the unrealized truth of every human being. Further, there is a common fallen nature all men have. All have sinned. All are lost. All are slaves to sin. Those truths are expressed in varying ways among the tribes of men. It is concluded that there is a common equal doom for all. There are now no tribes of men that have any advantage in salvation. Though in the process of history God used one nation to receive the advantages of the law, the Scriptures, the covenants, and to be the means of bringing Christ according to the flesh into the world, those advantages have all been negated. God has counted all in unbelief.

It is from there that the gospel of grace goes out and we begin to swim in the deep waters of Christology. In accordance with God's own purposes, there may yet be temporal advantages to our familial or national identity as to circumstances and opportunities. Yet, who you and I are in those terms does not matter. They make us no closer to Christ, give us no greater portion of the Spirit of God, and give us no aid in giving God glory. All who are saved by Christ are fellow partakers of a new created order.

> For the love of Christ constraineth us; because we thus judge, that if one died for all, then were all dead: And that he died for all, that they which live should not henceforth live unto themselves, but unto him which died for them, and rose again. Wherefore henceforth know we no man after the flesh: yea, though we have known Christ after the flesh, yet now henceforth know we him no more. Therefore if any man be in Christ, he is a new creature: old things are passed away; behold, all things are become new. (2 Cor 5:14–17)

Here an important textual question needs to be asked. What does Paul mean when he says that, from this point forward, we do not know any man after the flesh? The context tells us that this is a conclusion drawn from the death of Christ for all who are saved and the ethical imperative that we live for Him instead of ourselves. If there is an "order of loves," Christ trumps all other loves. What was once natural to our fallen nature becomes repugnant to us in this newly created order. Our place in Christ is to give us a new view and consideration of humanity as a whole and all individuals in it. Our natural fallen state took matters of race, class, station, familial advantages, color, and culture into account in matters of life. Christ changed everything. Our place in Christ does not mean that we cease to use our citizenship, cease to call our parents and siblings our own, or even act in matters of this life in accordance with our present culture when that does not contradict the law of Christ. What it does mean is that we cease from estimating any person in matters of Christ (or in related ways in our conduct in this world) after those categories. That means that in the church, we judge that all peoples, classes, races, and so on have equal access to the means of grace; that in ministry each is equally deserving of ministry; that in the matter of taking the gospel we are indebted to give to all. Christ is not for any particular race above others, any particular families above others, any particular class above others.

This matter was still explicitly connected to the gentile controversy in the days of Paul. As the gospel went forward it began to go to others outside of the Jewish people. This caused all manner of consternation to Jewish professors of faith. Some Jews in this sense believed that they were yet the advantaged people and not unclean like the others. This perception of uncleanness in the out-group made it difficult, if not impossible, to share equally in the things of Christ. This earned those that held such a view some of the strongest rebukes from the apostles (Gal 1:6–8). Such is the natural bent of our flesh to see our in-group as holding a special place.

Paul warns the reader to cease from seeing Christ in terms of the flesh, contrary to the tendency of racially driven cults. Everyone desires to have a Christ that represents their group. Though Christ came as a Jew after the flesh, this does not limit any from coming and sharing in Him fully. Despite the Jewish distinctions of His heritage, He is the Savior of all men. All who call Him Lord are His. James, who was brother to our Lord, considered himself just as much the servant of Christ as any other (Jas 1:1; 2:1). Paul rebukes without apology any thought that a genetic relationship has any spiritual significance. The genetics of Christ ceased to be a meaningful reality, for He has been made the Lord of all by the resurrection from the dead and we were made new creatures in that reality.

So it is that in this new vein of thought, where in Christ all are made alive, a Christian egalitarianism is proclaimed. Not an egalitarianism that sees no moral differences in fallen cultures, for one is relatively better off not to live in a culture that practices human sacrifice. Such an absolute leveling is farcical. Instead, a Christian egalitarianism sees an equality wrought by Christ for all who are subject to Him. There in Christ the fleshly distinctions that man holds as meaningful truly disappear. The only distinction that is truly meaningful is whether one is truly in Christ. If not found in Christ, any sense of racial pride is meaningless, for all are equally dead without Him and all who have life only find it in Him.

CHAPTER 7

The People Christ Saved

"Therefore if any man be in Christ, he is a new creature: old things are passed away; behold, all things are become new." 2 CORINTHIANS 5:17

WHEN THE SCRIPTURES SPOKE of the coming Christ, that He would save His people from their sins (Matt 1:21), the question must be asked, "Who are the people of Christ?" It is this people that Christ concerned Himself with in His mission to save, to sanctify, and to glorify.

> And we know that all things work together for good to them that love God, to them who are the called according to his purpose. For whom he did foreknow, he also did predestinate to be conformed to the image of his Son, that he might be the firstborn among many brethren. Moreover whom he did predestinate, them he also called: and whom he called, them he also justified: and whom he justified, them he also glorified. (Rom 8:28–30)

This "them" is the ones for "whom" Christ acted. They love God and are called by Him unto Himself. All of sovereignty worked for their good, and the purpose was to make them like Christ. They are His true family, brothers of Christ and children of God. Who are these people? What is this race?

In consideration of the people that Christ saved, a general and familiar problem needs to be overcome: the problem of walking by sight instead of by faith (2 Cor 5:7). There is a need to discern the body of Christ and that is done by faith (1 Cor 11:29).[1] Our natural inclination is to see ourselves as

1. Note that these words were spoken partly to address division by class, rich and

coming to the mountain that might be shaken instead of the heavenly Jerusalem where the spirits of righteous men made perfect are (Heb 12:18–28). We want to see our identity as stemming from those shakable and changeable things instead of the unseen realities. God has a people. Ruth realized this in type when she refused Moab and embraced Naomi's people as her people. Peter highlighted this truth when he spoke to those who had been born anew (1 Pet 1:3), who were begotten of the word of God (1 Pet 1:23):

> But ye are a chosen generation, a royal priesthood, an holy nation, a peculiar people; that ye should shew forth the praises of him who hath called you out of darkness into his marvellous light; Which in time past were not a people, but are now the people of God: which had not obtained mercy, but now have obtained mercy. (1 Pet 2:9–10)

As Christians, we are the people of God, citizens of His kingdom. Our lives are hidden with Christ in God (Col 3:3). Our country and citizenship is in heaven (Phil 3:20). Our lineage is Christ's lineage. According to Peter, we have gone from the state of spiritual darkness to living in God's marvelous light and from the state of not belonging to the people of God to having obtained mercy from God (1 Pet 2:9–10). Our natural heritage, no matter what sense of pride is felt in it, is one of darkness and alienation from God.

There has been much good ink spilled on notions of superior races and cultures. I will concede that a culture that puts an emphasis on Bible reading and prayer is superior to one that commits human sacrifices or ravages strangers. However, we are really comparing abstract entities at that point. The best of cultures are still sinful cultures. There never was a golden age of human society despite our mythmaking. That rhetoric does not fit what Peter said of our natural state. No matter what identity I find in that natural state, it is still lost. There is no significant difference to be found between our natural state and that of others. What are the nations, the races, the peoples of this world? They are but a drop in the bucket; they are lighter than vanity (Ps 62:9). So much pride is put in those genetic and cultural differences to cause foolish men to find all their worth and identity therein.

What is my race as it relates to my natural state? Right now, as I examine it in the light of the Scriptures, I find no greatness in it. I do not even find a static quality to it. I am the product of eight sets of great-great-grandparents and that only covers the last 150 years or so of my lineage. What do I know about them? I know little about most of them. I can say

---

poor, when taking of the Lord's Table.

that the culture they lived in is not the same culture I now live in. I also know that their culture was no more of a moral paragon than my own. I know little to nothing about them genetically speaking. I know that they left me with a hodgepodge of various genetic markers, all of which are just as perishing as those belonging to other men. I have no certain idea of my race by peering into their genetic lineage. Their generations produced just as much ungodliness as mine, though different in their manifestations.

If I narrow the question of my race to that patriarchal last name, I can say, "I am a Tackett." I know a little more about that one sixteenth part of my genetics.[2] I can track it back to the 1620s in Virginia, bearing what appeared to be a French spelling. Before that, I can trace *possible* ties to Ireland or to France with no definite knowledge either way. Anything great I wish to posit is likely fiction invented by myself or someone else. I do not know if they (most of them) were strong men or cowards, righteous men or lecherous. The romantic in me says that they were all great men, but again that is probably fiction. However, that patriarchal name contains things that I truly respect: for example, the adventurous spirit that brought me to where I am right now (at least a small portion of me). Yet when I look closer at them, there is vanity and sinfulness. I often joke that we Tacketts were either drunkards or preachers, and sometimes both at the same time. Sadly, the little that I do know about those that held that patriarchal name adds too much truth to that pun.

I might say that my race is American, whatever that happens to mean. I guess it means I am not Mexican or Canadian; I have my citizenship here and live under American laws. That would be the closest thing I have to the biblical concept of *ethnos*, like the idea of being Roman, Cretan, or Israeli. I can easily give myself over to patriotic feelings in this regard. Nevertheless, what is this idea of being an American? Does it give me some special status? Is it good? There are times that I consider the way my nation has shed innocent blood, exported wickedness and ungodliness to the ends of this earth, and has given way to shameless corruption that the moniker "American" ceases to be a source of pride. "Woe is me . . . I dwell in the midst of a people of unclean lips" (Isa 6:5). What nation or race is good and is capable in their nature alone of being called the people of God?

It may be said of all peoples that the heathen rage and seek to cast off the fetters of God and Christ (Ps 2). Luke applied that Scripture to both

2. Though the further back I go the smaller portion of genetic connection I have with the ones carrying that name.

Jew and Roman (Acts 4:25–28). It is equally true of my generation and my great-great-grandparents' generation. No matter what lens I look through, I belong to a people who are in darkness and are not God's people. What I have received from my name, my lineage, and national ties is what Peter said I need to be redeemed from, that is, the "vain conversation received by tradition from [my] fathers" (1 Pet 1:18).

Every culture only has as much light as it contains the light of Christ. Progressive theology has set the light of culture foolishly in man, believing that man will arrive at some golden age by himself and for himself. The news flows in daily that the light that is in each of us is darkness. How great is that darkness! Liberal and Marxists theologians have called the truth of Christ damnable colonialism and have called for its chains to be broken. However, they replace Him with heavier chains that bind men as slaves. There is not a shade or tint of humanity that does not stand in absolute need of the truth of Christ.

This tension between faith and sight regarding this matter was taken up by John the Baptist in his ministry, as we saw earlier. While preaching the message of repentance, he warned his hearers, "Bring forth therefore fruits worthy of repentance, and begin not to say within yourselves, we have Abraham to our father: for I say unto you, That God is able of these stones to raise up children unto Abraham" (Luke 3:8; see also Matt 3:9). Here, racial pride was adopted by a given people that became a barrier to repentance. Genetics and outward signs thereof meant to them that they had a special relationship with God. However, John told them that God can take from the inanimate things of this world and form other children for Himself, much as He did when He formed the first man and crowned him. Such a hyperbolic statement was intended to correct a false and foolish sense of racial superiority, and it did so succinctly.

The words of John point to the need to move (or be moved) from one state to another. Specifically, the word *egeiró* ("to raise up") speaks to this end. Christ was raised from death to life. Stones could be made by God to move from an inanimate state to the state of covenant relationship. Those people that stood before John needed repentance to move them from the state of being a physical son to being a true son of Abraham. The terms of the new covenant are just that: by grace one can go from the state of having a heart of stone (death) to the state of having a heart of flesh (life; Ezek 36:26). Racial pride is useless; the grace of God alone matters.

The ones who say "Abraham is our father" say nothing in that statement regarding a true relationship with God. The same may be said of the parable of the rich man and Lazarus. A central point of that parable is to highlight the difference between appearance and reality regarding one's true relationship to Abraham. This is a theme Christ took up elsewhere in direct teaching (John 8:39–40). In the parable, the unnamed rich man was unnamed for a reason, for he had no true relationship to the covenant. Lazarus was named because he did. As the parable unfolds, the rich man appears to have the blessings of riches, expensive clothing, and a gated home (likely in the promised land). The other appeared to lack the outward signs with no gate of his own, in company of dogs for comfort, and begging for sustenance. Yet Lazarus, whose name means "God has helped," died and was received into Abraham's bosom, while the rich man found no possible relationship to Abraham in death. The outward appearance of the rich man could not make up for the reality that there was no repentance at the word of God that alone was able to move him from one state to another. That was what he was told in the state of his torment.

The focus is wrong when it is placed on anything outside of the work of grace that God alone does. Christ said that you must be born again (John 3:3, 5). If I consider my race as my broad lineage, my patriarchal name, or my nation, I run into the cruel fact that it is filled with wicked men producing sinful and idolatrous cultures. My current godless culture was mostly produced by people with similar shades of skin as me, and it was allowed to fester by the same type of cowardly men who would not stand for the right in their time. While we can say that there are some cultures more just than others, it is laughable to believe that any culture has been made by man that is superior in its nature. The whole of human empires, whether they were of gold or iron mixed with clay, were and are crushed by the stone cut out of the mountain (Dan 2). I have my Abrahams and Jacobs in my lineage, from whom I have inherited great blessings, but their lives (like those biblical characters) cannot stand moral reckoning without grace. As I survey my race, I am left to confess as Daniel or Nehemiah did the great sinfulness of my fathers and of my nation from which preceded great guiltiness on us all. The sins of our culture are just as much the inheritance of our fathers as anything else. The weaknesses and injustices of our nation are an indictment against our race (or separate races). If it will be more tolerable for the men of Sodom than the men of Capernaum in the final judgment, will the same comparison yield the same result for ours (Matt 11:20–24)?

How are we superior in the final tally? One who holds to a sense of racial pride is holding on to an illusion. One can be grateful for the good things of one's fathers without falling into such folly.

"You must be born again." You need to be made a new creature in Christ. There is nothing in your heritage that can aid you before God. Maybe you have grown up in church and heard from the cradle the songs of Zion, but without the work of the Spirit of God you are as lost as the most barbarous brutes. You belong to a condemned race. In Adam all die. There are no exceptions. All cultures that proceed from Adam die. All families that belong to Adam die. "All nations before [God] are as nothing; and they are counted to him less than nothing, and vanity" (Isa 40:17). Where is the exception? God now "commandeth all men every where to repent" (Acts 17:30–31). All nations of men are destined to stand guilty before their God. There will be those that will be more condemned, but there are none that will stand less than condemned in Adam.

If the new birth is necessary, and it most certainly is, then our first birth is insufficient, no matter how noble we hold it to be. In the insufficiency of our natural birth the ground is leveled and there is equal doom for all. The new birth and authority to be called the sons of God is applicable to any that will receive Christ and believe in His name (John 1:12). The message of Isaiah was pointed, which was quoted by Christ near the time He pronounced the desolation of the house of Israel. All who will receive the word and do it will be counted as His people. Christ says that even the sons of strangers will be among His own.

> Even them will I bring to my holy mountain, and make them joyful in my house of prayer: their burnt offerings and their sacrifices shall be accepted upon mine altar; for mine house shall be called an house of prayer for all people. The Lord GOD which gathereth the outcasts of Israel saith, Yet will I gather others to him, beside those that are gathered unto him. (Isa 56:7–8)

There is an impassable gulf that is crossed by God as He takes any who are lost from the state of not being His people to being the sons of the living God. This great miracle is called regeneration.

Nicodemus was told of this necessity of regeneration. "Verily, verily, I say unto thee, Except a man be born of water and of the Spirit, he cannot enter into the kingdom of God" (John 3:5). The context begins two verses earlier when Christ says that unless one is born *anóthen* they cannot see the kingdom of God. That word means either "from above" or "anew"—meaning that there must be some kind of heavenly birth in order for one to relate in any way to the heavenly kingdom. The first birth, the natural birth, will not suffice. This caused for Nicodemus to make an absurd conclusion, thinking that Christ is speaking of a second natural birth, entering a second time into the womb of the mother. Christ in answer speaks of two separate types of birth, a birth of water and (separated by the conjunction *kai*) also a birth of the Spirit. The context demands that Christ's explanation is of the difference between the first and second birth, the natural and supernatural. Whatever water is intended to mean, it answers to one's natural birth which is insufficient without the supernatural birth. This becomes even more apparent as the dichotomy between flesh and spirit are brought out again in the next verse: "That which is born of the flesh is flesh; and that which is born of the Spirit is spirit" (John 3:6). The dichotomous thought is consistently being applied. The first birth, the natural birth, the water birth, is that which is of the flesh. This is true no matter what one's color is, their family name, or their place of birth. The second birth, the supernatural or from above birth, the birth of the Spirit, is what is of the spiritual world. The likely meaning that fits the duality of the context is that water represents the water of the mother's womb. Christ is distinguishing the work of the Spirit, which happens without observation, apart from the world of sight. Ultimately, it is the Spirit of God working faith that brings forth salvation in the broader context (John 3:15–16).

For Nicodemus, an Israelite, who had waited all his life for this kingdom to come, that he may rule and reign with the Messiah, the Son of David, to hear such was unbearable. Jesus told them that unless each individual had this experience, they would never see it.

Peter adds to the teaching of the new birth stating that the "God and Father of our Lord Jesus Christ . . . according to his abundant mercy hath begotten us again unto a lively hope by the resurrection of Jesus Christ from the dead" (1 Pet 1:3). The use of the Greek genitive points us to the resurrection of Christ as the means of bringing the new birth to pass. Christ is our regeneration, the firstborn from the dead (Col 1:18). He is the firstborn of the new creation (Col 1:15). He did what saves us from our life in Adam where all die. Peter again said, "[We are] born again, not of corruptible seed, but of incorruptible, by the word of God, which liveth and abideth for ever" (1 Pet 1:23). The context tells us that the blood of the Lamb and not silver and gold received by the tradition of our fathers redeems us (1 Pet 1:18). Nothing about who we are according to the flesh is worthy to be mentioned in this entire vein of theological truth. Our fathers gave us silver and gold idols, unable to save. We need the word of God to change us, and that word is the gospel of Christ, what He did on our behalf (1 Pet 1:23–25).

John in his prologue was even more forthright. Regeneration is not an operation performed by men, even holy men, and it is not something that flows in any way from our natural life.

> He came unto his own, and his own received him not. But as many as received him, to them gave he power to become the sons of God, even to them that believe on his name: Which were born, not of blood, nor of the will of the flesh, nor of the will of man, but of God. (John 1:11–13)

Regeneration is something that God does by His own will for the believing. It is to "as many as received Him" or believed in the name of Christ that the right to be called the sons of God is given (John 1:12). The reality of repentance and faith flows from the sovereign and monergistic work of regeneration. Those who believe are indeed those that are born of God, and they are so born solely by the operation of God.

Three truths are excluded from connection with regeneration in John's prologue. The first of these is directly related to the subject of race. Regeneration is not of blood or, rather, it is outside of any connection to human descent. Salvation is not founded on who our parents or forefathers are.[3] Being the children of Abraham was not enough to prepare the Pharisees for baptism. They were rather told that their boast of having Abraham as their natural father was superfluous. New children could come from the very rocks. Salvation not being of blood strikes hard at man's basic pride. There are many in this world counting on guidance from their ancestors to bring them into the unseen world. Several cults have sprung up believing

3. It could be questioned here whether baptism as a picture of regeneration is applicable to the often-touted idea of "covenant children." If infants are "holy" by virtue of being the children of believers and therefore are subject to baptism as a sign of regeneration (as opposed to being holy in the sense of being products of a legitimate marriage; 1 Cor 7:13–15), then John 1:12–13 would seem to be superfluous and contradictory. However, regarding the concept of "covenant children" as textually drawn out by its proponents from Luke's words in Acts 2:38–39, the concept appears to be in error. The new covenant promise of the Spirit is rather the concept of the gospel going to the Jew first (i.e., Israel; Jer 31:33—that is, "to you and your children") and then to the gentile (i.e., "and to all that are afar off"). All of these are those who are called to repent and receive the promise, "as many as the Lord our God shall call." It does not establish "covenant children" who are somehow saved by blood in contradiction to John's prologue, but rather that God saves both Jew and Gentile alike.

that their ethnic ties (real or imagined) make them covenant members of God's family. They are living in direct contradiction to the plain reading of the Scriptures. As long as they hold on to such delusions, they know nothing of the new birth. They, regardless of their pedigree, are still in Adam where all die.

This does not mean that there should be a lack of honor and respect for one's godly heritage or even an admiration for what our ancestors have accomplished. I am proud (in the sense of counting myself blessed) of specific members of my family that preceded me. My father was a faithful pastor and two of his siblings served faithfully as missionaries and evangelists. My grandfather gave his life to planting churches. My great-grandfather served faithfully as moderator of the old Regular Baptist in Eastern Kentucky. That is immediately meaningful to me. Nevertheless, it does nothing for me before God. On the contrary, I found myself at the age of twenty-one lost and without Christ. Nothing about my life in Christ is found in those ties. Righteousness is something that is received, not handed down through our parents, like genetic markers or family Bibles. For instance, Paul repudiated his culture and heritage that he might be found in Christ (Phil 3:3–11). There was no place for him to have "confidence in the flesh." The only thing I have received from the blood of my heritage related to new life in Christ is sin and death that were passed down throughout all generations (Rom 5:12). The sentence of death is upon all men, for we are all sinners from birth. We are shaped in iniquity and conceived in sin.

John continues to speak of regeneration as an operation of God alone, mitigating any sense that man in any way produces it. Since these other elements do not directly relate to our topic of race, a brief summary will suffice. The new birth is not something accomplished by "the will of the flesh." In other words, it does not derive from human design. It is not an act we do or devise to do that brings about the new birth. Isaiah said, "All our righteousness are as filthy rags" (Isa 64:6).

Regeneration as an operation of God is also not of "the will of men." Salvation does not come by corporate human desire. John ruled out the administrator of salvation being any organization of men doing anything which results in the new birth. Religious institutions cannot save, in whole or in part, by their deeds or by their participation with God. What a priest or pastor does in the baptismal waters is not synonymous with the new birth. The reality of salvation is not synonymous with any act administered by men. There is a false notion in contemporary church practice that we can create conditions by which the lost can be brought to salvation. However, salvation rests wholly on the will of God (John 3:8; Jas 1:18). Though hand joins in hand, the sinner will yet be punished (Prov 11:21).

We know from the Scriptures that regeneration is an operation of God obtained by faith. It is known solely by its result: the one believing is born of God. It is not from genetics, the individual human will, or collective human effort. Salvation is of the Lord. God has chosen to save some out of the pitiful condition of our humanity. That choice of God to save was free from all consideration of race, relative goodness, or cultural acumen. Anyone who tries to fit any of those tenets into salvation does so contrary to the Scriptures. God has considered those things vain. He chooses whom He will save from that vanity; He is not a respecter of persons (Acts 10:34).

So who did He choose to save? He chose to save whoever, any. To say it in a more exact way, God has not limited His choice to save based on anything in or of man. We cannot point to any human characteristic and say, "That is what makes one saveable in the eyes of God." The fact that Isaac and Ishmael were both children of Abraham made no difference to God when He chose Isaac over Ishmael. The fact that Jacob and Esau were carried in the same womb, born into the same culture, made no difference to God. The fact that Isaac desired to make Esau the firstborn made no difference. God freely chose the one and rejected the other. The one believing in Christ and receiving Him, whoever that may be, is one that has been born of God. Was there anything special about the remnant that caused God to keep them from bowing to Baal (Rom 11:4)? No, there was nothing special about any of them when compared to others. They were Israelites just like the other idolaters, but God chose to keep them from idolatry.

Christ made a similar argument for grace being given outside of the people of Israel in the context of the Jews of Nazareth rejecting Him as Messiah:

> But I tell you of a truth, many widows were in Israel in the days of Elias, when the heaven was shut up three years and six months, when great famine was throughout all the land; But unto none of them was Elias sent, save unto Sarepta, a city of Sidon, unto a woman that was a widow. And many lepers were in Israel in the time of Eliseus the prophet; and none of them was cleansed, saving Naaman the Syrian. (Luke 4:25–27)

This doctrine of the freedom of God to choose to save whoever He pleases to save is often met with anger by those who feel like their position is favorable to God and should be considered. It was like that as Christ said the above words. They became angry that He pointed out that God not only chooses who He will have mercy on, but He also gave grace to hated gentiles (Luke 4:28–29).

This continued to be played out in the rest of the New Testament. The gentile centurion was declared by Christ to have a great faith not found in Israel, and then Christ declared:

> And I say unto you, That many shall come from the east and west, and shall sit down with Abraham, and Isaac, and Jacob, in the kingdom of heaven. But the children of the kingdom shall be cast out into outer darkness: there shall be weeping and gnashing of teeth. (Matt 8:11–12)

There would be many according to Christ that had no favored status in the sight of others but would be objects of mercy and examples of faith. Those would take part in all the promises of God's chosen people while those that felt that race gave them such rights would be cast out.

These "whoever" people are freely chosen by God for salvation and are the true people of God. There is no tribe or class of people that God has chosen to exclude from His electing and saving work, His covenant of redemption. Christ spoke of these "whoever" people as being "all that the Father has given to [Christ]" (John 6:37). What do those words tell us? They tell us that the choice of God to save the "whoever" freely, without respect to who they are or what they do, without any revealed boundary or distinction, was in the heart of the Father prior to the incarnation of Christ and prior to the existence of any national divisions. We would call this prelapsarian, prior to the fall in the mind of God. It was before the foundation of the world that the Father gave a people to the Son (Eph 1:4). It is these people the Son purposed to redeem, who were written before the foundation of the world in the Lamb's book of life (Rev 17:8).

These people that the Father chose and were given to the Son are declared by Christ to have a particular truth about them: "All that the Father giveth me shall come to me" (John 6:37). The giving of the Father to the Son as a whole was logically prior to their coming to Christ. This is the doctrine of election. It also provides a definite identity to who the elect of God are. The elect of God are those who come to Christ.

In the indefiniteness of their identity, they are fully secured in the salvation of God: "Him that cometh to me I will in no wise cast out" (John 6:37). This "whoever" that comes to Christ will forever be held by

Christ. They will under no circumstance ever be cast out. That is called the doctrine of preservation. They will be fully saved in the end: "All which he hath given me I should lose nothing, but should raise it up again at the last day" (John 6:39). If salvation was based on something other than the free election of God, then some external idea or factor could identify these people. One would simply know that people who had this culture or these genetic markers were given to Christ and are the people of Christ. Christ laid the identity of this people rather in the free choice of the Father (whoever He chose to give to the Son) and marked them with complete indefiniteness (whoever comes to the Son). This *coming* is given greater fullness in context as being synonymous with *believing* (John 3:35, 40).

Again, the truth becomes apparent in New Testament doctrine that these people are those who are brought from one state to another. There was a time that these people were yet in Adam and by the work of salvation were translated into Christ. They were dead and then they were quickened (Eph 2:1). They were without Christ and without hope, and then they were brought nigh to Christ (Eph 2:12–14). They went from not being a people to being the people of God. This paradigm makes the status of being part of the people of God solely a matter of mercy and grace. It flows from the Father, through the efficacious work of Christ, and then to the believer (by means of the Spirit)—the passive receiver of such great mercy. The Son was given those who were yet under the righteous wrath of God. He stood as their priest offering up Himself for them, securing their salvation thereby.

> And every priest standeth daily ministering and offering oftentimes the same sacrifices, which can never take away sins: But this man, after he had offered one sacrifice for sins for ever, sat down on the right hand of God; From henceforth expecting till his enemies be made his footstool. For by one offering he hath perfected for ever them that are sanctified. Whereof the Holy Ghost also is a witness to us: for after that he had said before, This is the covenant that I will make with them after those days, saith the Lord, I will put my laws into their hearts, and in their minds will I write them; And their sins and iniquities will I remember no more. (Heb 10:11–17)

Christ did not make salvation possible by His cross but actually saved all who are saved by it. Christ represented all who are saved and perfectly sanctified them as their High Priest. This work effectively makes them holy unto God and secure members of the new covenant, where their sins will be remembered no more. Again, there is nothing here definitely known about the elect other than they are those people that Christ represented in His High Priestly office. Christ has already perfected (*teleioó*—in the perfect tense) those (indefinitely described with a present participle) that are being sanctified (*hagiazó*). Those coming to Christ find that Christ has already perfected their salvation, whoever they may be.

This matter of entering the covenant contains the truth that these people were outside of the covenant and then are brought in by Christ. It is the New Testament ratified by the offering of the blood of Christ (Matt 26:28). Israel in her sin could not keep the former covenant but broke it, and in grace the new covenant was promised (Jer 31:31–34). Those natural branches having been broken off are yet able by grace alone to be grafted back into the greater reality of the new covenant. In reality, no one now has any connection to the promises, at least not in Adam (see chapter 6). To the Jew and gentile alike, God has said, "You are not my people," and from that truth Christ says to the elect (whoever that may be), "You are sons of the living God" (1 Pet 2:9–10).

This transformation only appears to be more pronounced when speaking of those who were gentiles. What Hosea prophesied first to Israel, Paul applied to all the elect. It included the gentile converts, who were not the people of God too (Hos 1:10; Rom 9:23–26; 1 Pet 2:9–10). The gospel going out to the gentiles outside of the old covenant became the great scandal in the New Testament. Gentiles before the gospel had nothing to connect them at all to any covenant of God, unlike Israel. Jews could boast that they were circumcised as a sign of their race having a covenant with the living God. The unbelieving Jews foolishly took their circumcision to be a real connection to a spiritual reality and the uncircumcision of the gentile as a sign of an unsanctified nature (Rom 2:29). They saw the gentile as completely foreign from God (Eph 2:11–12).

Paul describes believing gentiles as becoming part of God's covenant people by being joined to Christ, despite their lack of all outward signs. In the second chapter to the Colossians, Paul spoke in the most wonderful terms to these gentile believers. He said that they were "dead in [their] sins and the uncircumcision of [their] flesh, [and then in Christ being] quickened together with him, having [been] forgiven all trespasses" (Col 2:13). Christ alone did this. He made those who were uncircumcised "circumcised with the circumcision made without hands, in putting off the body of the sins of the flesh by the circumcision of Christ" (Col 2:11). In other words, they who were not His covenant people and had no outward signs of being so, because of what Christ did on the cross and in His ascension, now are counted as circumcised. The death of Christ was the only circumcision that they would need. They were grafted into all the promises of life, inheritance, title, and blessings (Rom 11). By that they are now "buried with him in baptism [a reference to His death], wherein also [they] are risen with him through the faith of the operation of God, who hath raised him from the dead" (Col 2:12). Because they are in Christ, they now have life (Gal 2:20). They are no longer in Adam, where all die, but in Christ—dead, buried, and living with resurrected life. Despite in the flesh being called something to the contrary, they are circumcised in heart through the operation of God through Christ. They are forgiven because He took the accusation of their death upon Himself (Col 2:13–14).

Paul reiterated this truth to the Ephesians as the great mystery of the gospel committed to him:

> For this cause I Paul, the prisoner of Jesus Christ for you Gentiles, If ye have heard of the dispensation of the grace of God which is given me to you-ward: How that by revelation he made known unto me the mystery; (as I wrote afore in few words, Whereby, when ye read, ye may understand my knowledge in the mystery of Christ) Which in other ages was not made known unto the sons of men, as it is now revealed unto his holy apostles and prophets by the Spirit; That the Gentiles should be fellowheirs, and of the same body, and partakers of his promise in Christ by the gospel: Whereof I was made a minister, according to the gift of the grace of God given unto me by the effectual working of his power. Unto me, who am less than the least of all saints, is this grace given, that I should preach among the Gentiles the unsearchable riches of Christ; And to make all *men* see what *is* the fellowship of the mystery, which from the beginning of the world hath been hid in God, who created all things by Jesus Christ: To the intent that now unto the principalities and powers in heavenly *places* might be known by the church the manifold wisdom of God, According to the eternal purpose which he purposed in Christ Jesus our Lord: In whom we have boldness and access with confidence by the faith of him. (Eph 3:1–12)

Here is a precious truth. Every nation where the gospel goes, those who believe on it become fellow heirs. They become equals with the believing Jews. They become one with Christ and one with one another. Those that are in Christ are the new people of God, the one new humanity (Eph 2:15).

They who do not have Christ are not the people of God. They have no connection with the promises.

There is one people of God with perfect equality. The nature of man, Jew or gentile alike, is not sufficient. The name of the dead stands in need of redemption. As a Moabite woman among God's people, there was no hold that Ruth had on God. If it was not for the grace given through levirate marriage to raise up the name of the dead she would have perished. The valley of dry bones could not live until God through His word brought life to them (Ezek 37:1–14). Broken branches and branches having no natural connection to the covenant of God have the same outcome if grace does not graft them into the covenant promises.

The narrative of Acts begins in Jerusalem and ends in Rome. It moves from the 144,000 Israelites to the innumerable multitude from every race. The narrative of the New Testament pointed to unfinished missionary work yet beyond the book of Acts (to Spain and beyond). The gospel that was first preached in Jerusalem was intended to go everywhere. "To the Jew first" was not a matter of preeminence but process, with no boundaries of nation or race or tribe. God has a people and, as the gospel penetrates further into the world, He is calling that people to Himself. The gospel goes out to "whoever."

> For the scripture saith, Whosoever believeth on him shall not be ashamed. For there is no difference between the Jew and the Greek: for the same Lord over all is rich unto all that call upon him. (Rom 10:11–12)

CHAPTER 8

The People Christ Is Saving

"For ye are all the children of God by faith in Christ Jesus. For as many of you as have been baptized into Christ have put on Christ. There is neither Jew nor Greek, there is neither bond nor free, there is neither male nor female: for ye are all one in Christ Jesus. And if ye be Christ's, then are ye Abraham's seed, and heirs according to the promise." GALATIANS 3:26–29

PAUL CONDEMNED THE DECLARATION of a false gospel that was embraced by many Galatians, and at the heart of that false gospel was a division of race as it related to the sanctification of believers (Gal 1). In the Jerusalem Council (Acts 15), the formal question was this—what was necessary for gentiles (*ethnos*), non-Israelites, to do after believing in Christ? At the heart of this controversy was a battle for the interpretation of the Great Commission and true discipleship (Matt 28:18–20). There were those that believed that if the gentiles were not circumcised and did not begin to follow the dietary and ceremonial laws of cleanness (which at that time were only able to be kept by ethnic Jews) that they could not be true disciples. The historical narrative of the Jerusalem Council ended with apostles agreeing that there was no such necessity in the sanctifying work of the gentiles.[1]

Further teaching from the apostles made it clearer that there were not two levels of sanctification. First, there is no apostolic expectation that the customs of the gentiles in table fellowship with the Jews would make either unclean (See Gal 1, 2). Then, the matter of culture and customs themselves

1. See Tackett, *Sex and the Gospel*, 35–54, Antithesis 3.

(e.g., the keeping of days and diets) were left as a matter of personal conviction, and not something to judge one another over or break necessary fellowship (see Rom 14). The judgment of the new covenant Scriptures is that race and ethnicity have no special role in the sanctification of any Christian. The broader principle that needs to be applied is this—anyone who makes a racial distinction in the matter of sanctification is in danger of teaching a false gospel. That principle needs to be repeated often—any race-based faith immediately falls into this great danger. It might manifest itself in Christian Identity cults that say it is necessary for "Whites" to keep certain laws as part of their identity, but not necessary for "lesser races" to do so in whatever share in gospel promises they can enjoy. It may manifest itself in realist doctrines that say "non-Whites" are not even capable of being as sanctified as "Whites." These examples could easily be flipped to opposite contexts. Constructionists in critical race theory application elevate the "lived experiences" of "oppressed populations" over the "favored" as being more authentic and more meaningful. The end result of these false ideas of sanctification is that the gospel as it is lived out means something to one group that it does not mean to another group, based solely on race. Such are false gospels.

The tendency of fallen men is toward division and toward the maintenance of divisions, justifying their in-group/out-group preferences by any means. This is as true in political spaces as it is on the grade school playground. In terms of race, the divisions in our current culture tend to be justified by two differing sets of false premises. There are those that hold to an outcome-based divider and those that hold to a source divider. These two are active errors always attempting to infiltrate the church of God.

The outcome-based divider is the basis of what is now called critical theory. It begins with the premise that what we call race is a social construct.[2] According to this social construct ideology, man creates societal structures that favor their own people group over others. Those outcomes create disparities among groups. While there is a little truth here, the error is its dismissing of God's activity and pressing all differences into the single variable of human action. Therefore, to remedy those man-created disparities, via a Marxist call for leveling, revolutionaries are called upon to demolish current societal structures. A mechanism included in that revolution is

2. Instead of seeing race as divinely appointed differences among men—God actively in history creating national boundaries and causing, by blessing or diminishing for His various purposes, one *ethnos* to differ one from another.

adoption of new structures that remove favor from the "favored" group and give that favor instead to the "oppressed" group, a Robin-Hood-like fairy tale. It is readily apparent who the god of this ideology is: man is the creator and savior of himself. This idolatry is clear, and its end is destruction, just as it is with all false gods. The outcome-based distinctions become fodder for creating more distinctions.[3] This false idea of salvation does not promote unity but an inordinate focus on dismantling real or imagined signs of favor, breeding hatred, envy, and covetousness one against another. Outcome-based dividers are used by constructionists to draw their fundamental belief in equality of outcomes toward Marxist utopian ends.

On the other end of the perceived political spectrum is a more insidious divider, a source divider. Realism in its recognition of race (as opposed to constructionism above) sees race as a biological reality and all culture springing from race. They are fond of saying, "Culture is downstream of race," when highlighting proposed evils of those not like them. The false premises of realism are as follows:

A. God created race as a biological reality.[4]

B. These biological group differences produce differences of ability (intellectually, physically, spiritually, etc.) that can be expressed as having superior or inferior qualities.

C. Those cultures that are produced by various races reflect the superiority or inferiority of the races that produce them.

We can call these premises source dividers because, unlike constructionism, its basic assertion is that emerging inequalities come from the source of racial realities. Their view of God is not like that of the Scriptures, but more like classic deism whereby history is moved by nature that was only set in motion by God. Those that hold to such views rely heavily on supposed observations of "natural law," as opposed to a scriptural starting point. For instance, they will tout despairing crime statistics for one group, Intelligence Quotient data for another, and so on. They do not usually care to measure moral weaknesses in their own group, isolated parts of their own group that share those same disparities, and so on. They also do not

3. For an overview of critical theory see Baucham, *Fault Lines*.

4. They believe that each race indicates a differing "kind"—instead of God working historically by setting boundaries for nations, diminishing some and blessing others for His own purposes. It is never clear in their ideologies when these "created" realities were actualized by God.

care to apply the scriptural truths dealt with thus far. This is a great ignorance that Calvin warned against: "Whosoever, therefore, gives heed to those teachers who merely employ us in contemplating our good qualities, so far from making progress in self-knowledge, will be plunged into the most pernicious ignorance."[5]

Like the outcome-based divider, this source divider leaves little room for differing groups to consider one another their fellow heirs and equal brothers in Christ in the church. Instead of being divided by envy over perceived favored outcomes like the constructionist, they are divided by perceived racial and cultural superiority. In other words, they become divided by pride instead of being divided by envy or covetousness. It is normal rhetoric for realists to say that there is no place for unity of fellowship, equality of sanctification, or mutual benefit of service among the people of God where differing group representatives are present (though not all would be willing to take their belief to that conclusion). The realist in this sense is much more aligned with the Darwinist view of favored and disfavored races: in judging the capabilities of others, their worth in society, and desire to keep the divisions of kinds in place for the supposed health of their own racial group.

As to unscriptural division, the similarity in constructionism and realism is uncanny. Like the Judaizers of old with their false gospel, they demand that fellowship with the other can only be had if the other becomes one of them (if possible, at all). The constructionist will tell the "favored" to repent of their "favor" and then to take place as a second-class member of their group. The realist will tell the "inferior" to repent of their "inferior culture" and become a second-class member of theirs, if welcomed at all. Both are damnable heresies.

The Pharisee prayed and thanked God that he was not like others. He perceived that he was morally superior in his source (i.e., "not like other men") and in outcomes (i.e., "not like this publican"). Such pride divorced the Pharisee from the status of justification that the humbled publican had obtained (Luke 18:9–14).

Paul asked, "Who maketh you to differ from another?" (1 Cor 4:7) There are differences, varying strengths and weaknesses on a relative level, between us all. The Lord gives differing gifts for His glory and not the glory of the individual or group. All these differing gifts are to be used for the health of the whole body of believers (1 Cor 12:4–30). Instead of

5. Calvin, *Institutes of the Christian Religion* 2.1.282.

being reasons for separation, those differences become means of unity and growth. The eye cannot say that it has no need of the other members. The toe has no reason to say that since it is not the mouth it cannot be part of the body. Each part exists to edify the other members for the glory of God. Simply pointing out differences among individuals or groups does not establish that no unity among them can be had, strived for, or desired among the people of God. Such is certainly part of God's design.

Both realism and constructionism alike promote essential disunity, which perpetuates sinful attitudes toward others based on race. They create a tiered humanity and a tiered Christianity that denies the basic truths of the gospel. Racial identity does not merit grace (a contradiction of terms) but rather is something from which all need to be saved. One is not naturally in Christ but in Adam. All are by nature only the children of wrath (Eph 2:2–3). Whatever their race, they are under sin. Unredeemed culture is not downstream of race but downstream of man's fallenness. Whatever advantages race appears to give are nil. Again, we must be born again. To reinsert some form of importance to one's natural race in living out the Christian life is to set up what was abolished by Christ (Eph 2:14). It is idolatry. "This only would I learn of you, received ye the Spirit by the works of the law, or by the hearing of faith? Are ye so foolish? having begun in the Spirit, are ye now made perfect by the flesh?" (Gal 3:2–3) Rather, the Christian is called on to view themselves as part of a new people: a royal priesthood, a holy nation (1 Pet 2:9). Christians are together one new humanity in Christ (Eph 2:15). They are called on to see themselves as part of the race of Christ, together with all others that are also in Christ (regardless of their natural race); in unity, growing up together into the stature of Christ (Eph 4).

As it is related to living out the Christian life, the translation from our natural state to our spiritual state is what is before us at this point. We live out our Christian life in this world as Christians and not as White, or Black, or Jew, and so on. Every Christian is now our brother, and every unbeliever is now our mission field, where we represent Christ in calling them to faith. Christ becomes the whole of our identity in this world. As He is, so are we in this world (1 John 4:17). Consider this truth introduced by Paul:

> Moreover, brethren, I would not that ye should be ignorant, how that all our fathers were under the cloud, and all passed through the sea; And were all baptized unto Moses in the cloud and in the sea; And did all eat the same spiritual meat; And did all drink the

> same spiritual drink: for they drank of that spiritual Rock that followed them: and that Rock was Christ. (1 Cor 10:1–4)

Paul in this interesting narrative is speaking to a mostly gentile audience. He tells them that they were all in the wilderness, passing through the Red Sea, eating manna and drinking from the Rock. However, these were descriptions of ancient Israel at and after the exodus under the old covenant. The Corinthians were not Jews by lineage. Though they had no natural connection to the ancient nation of Israel, they had a true relationship with the people of God throughout time because they have spiritually partaken of Christ. This is where the theological language of Paul regarding gentiles being grafted in meets its practical application. In Christ, the fathers of the faith are the fathers of the gentiles too. Through various apostasies, there were always among Israel true Jews circumcised in heart. The covenant with them was never limited to "nature," for even the servants bought with money could enter that covenant, as it was when Abraham was first circumcised with all his family and existing servants (Gen 17:11–13; Exod 12:24).

In a sense, Paul is reminding the Corinthians of their true status. Paul and Sosthenes were writing to the people of God there at Corinth, people who were considered brothers in Christ though gentiles according to the flesh (1 Cor 1:1–2). "Nature" is seen in the twelfth chapter where Paul tells the Corinthians, "Ye know that ye were gentiles, carried away unto these dumb idols, even as ye were led" (1 Cor 12:2). There is only one possible sense of the Greek word *ethnos* (translated as "gentile") in this context: it is a non-Israelite. It would make no sense to say to them, "You were nationalities," or "You were political entities," or so on. The meaning was clear that at one point they were not part of the people of God: they were worshipers of false gods and alienated from the one true God. They were outside of the covenant nation of Israel. In the context of Corinthians, they who were of other nations became equal members of the body of Christ (1 Cor 12). They were outside of the commonwealth of Israel. The point of interest is the imperfect verb. They *were* gentiles; they *are* now in Christ and partakers of all that is true of Christ. Their natural identity, at least as it relates to their place in the church, was no longer their true identity.[6] Something greater now identified them and connected them with the household of faith.

6. Here we make passing mention of an objection. Being in Christ while still in the present world is not a complete repudiation of our earthly lineage or nationality. Paul still claimed Roman citizenship as he used it to navigate politically in this world and still

This is that mystery Paul spoke of in the third chapter to the Letter to the Ephesians. We are touching on a mystery revealed in Christ: both Jews and gentiles are now in one body and fellow heirs of God. Paul in connecting the Corinthian gentiles with the exodus gave them a real spiritual connection to salvific history, the same salvific history shared by their Jewish brothers. One does not have a greater connection to the history of faith than the other. Those that hold to a dispensational theology are fond of saying that the present "church age" where gentiles are grafted in is "parenthetical" to God's overall plan with the nation of Israel. That is not the theology of Paul. The gentiles who are brought close by Christ are fully connected with the whole of redemptive history. Despite their race, they are part of what God wrought in history that culminated with Christ. When they sat at the table of the Lord, taking the bread and wine which is the body of Christ, they were made partakers of the true exodus. True believers in the historical exodus drank of that spiritual rock that followed them, and that Rock was Christ. They shared the same Savior.

To the gentiles in Galatia, Paul brought forth the same truth. Paul said that the blessing of Abraham may come on the gentiles through Jesus Christ (Gal 3:14—again the obvious meaning of *ethnos* is "non-Israelite"). What is the blessing of Abraham? We are blessed in and through his seed, from whom God's blessings come upon all the nations of the earth (Gen 12:1–3). "Now to Abraham and his seed were the promises made. He saith not, and to seeds, as of many; but as of one, and to thy seed, which is Christ" (Gal 3:16). From there, Paul argues that the gentiles in Christ are no longer gentiles and that the same is true of the Jews in Christ. All, both Jews and gentiles, male and female, who are baptized into Christ, have put on Christ. We all represent Christ together in this world. We are all children of God by faith in Christ and not due to any factor in our physical disposition. In the sense of our salvation and sanctification in this world, there is now neither Jew nor Greek, male nor female. We are all equally[7] connected with the seed of Abraham and therefore are all partakers of the present and future blessings that such entails. If we are in Christ, then we are Abraham's seed, and heirs according to the promise (Gal 3:29). Thus, Paul spoke to gentiles and told

---

said he had a strong desire to see his brothers according to the flesh saved. He even gave tribute to that nation.

7. This is so while in the natural world and our life therein there are yet national realities and male and female roles.

them that they had part in the exodus. In Christ, His past is our past. It was God's Son who was truly called out of Egypt (Hos 11:1; Matt 2:15).

For a clearer instance of this truth, the second chapter in the Letter to the Ephesians is considered. Paul says to the gentile believers in Ephesus:

> Wherefore remember, that ye being in time past Gentiles in the flesh, who are called Uncircumcision by that which is called the Circumcision in the flesh made by hands; That at that time ye were without Christ, being aliens from the commonwealth of Israel, and strangers from the covenants of promise, having no hope, and without God in the world. (Eph 2:11–12)

There is clearly no other possible understanding of the word *ethnos* here other than a non-Israelite. They did not have the true God; they never had a part of the covenants and were never identified with the Israeli commonwealth. Yet Paul says to them:

> But now in Christ Jesus ye who sometimes were far off are made nigh by the blood of Christ. For he is our peace, who hath made both one, and hath broken down the middle wall of partition between us; Having abolished in his flesh the enmity, even the law of commandments contained in ordinances; for to make in himself of twain one new man, so making peace; And that he might reconcile both unto God in one body by the cross, having slain the enmity thereby: And came and preached peace to you which were afar off, and to them that were nigh. For through him we both have access by one Spirit unto the Father. Now therefore ye are no more strangers and foreigners, but fellowcitizens with the saints, and of the household of God; And are built upon the foundation of the apostles and prophets, Jesus Christ himself being the chief corner stone; In whom all the building fitly framed together groweth unto an holy temple in the Lord: In whom ye also are builded together for an habitation of God through the Spirit. (Eph 2:13–22)

Those who previously had no connection racially to the things of God are now full possessors of all things in Christ, having full access and growing into the temple of God together. They are not inferior in the sanctifying work done right now in the worship and glorifying of God through the Holy Spirit. We see the truth again that they *were* gentiles (just as the Galatians and Corinthians) but now they *are* something different and far greater. Their identity is now Christ and not their former Adamic race, whatever manifestation that may have been.

This is not some form of radical egalitarianism that says there are no distinctions that can be made, no systems of authority established, or no differences in administration or gifts among the people of God. What this doctrine contains is the conviction that those in Christ are equally members of the body of Christ and equally being used in the church for the mutual health and growth of other believers. The church increases by that which every joint supplies (Eph 4:16). What is connected to the olive tree bears fruit and they can only be connected to that olive tree by being grafted in by grace through faith (Rom 11). The natural branches (Israel) who were broken off due to unbelief and the unnatural branches not grafted in share in that same disposition and end (i.e., lifelessness). However, when either by faith are grafted in, then they are equally partakers of the tree and its life-giving root. There is no impediment in the church of God to full fellowship and participation in all aspects of the work of Christ for all, regardless of race.

Here is a minor point of contention with many of my faithful covenantal brethren. The accusation often wrongly hurled is that covenant theology teaches a replacement theology. That is, it is believed by some that covenant theology asserts that the physical nation of Israel was replaced by the church as the people of God. To the contrary, covenant theology teaches that there is one people of God, the church, of which the nation of Israel was a visible manifestation of that people (the true believing remnant among them being the true people of God), and the visible New Testament church is now the visible manifestation (the true believing among it being the true church or people of God). Again, Israel was the natural branches who, due to corporate unbelief, were broken off from those covenants. The gentile nations (those that believe among them) are the wild branches grafted in along with any of the believing Jews. Where the language of this breaks down and is made to sound like replacement theology is for covenant theologians to claim that the church *is* Israel, leading some to believe that they are claiming that the church is the natural branches. Israel is and was a physical nation of this world with an earthly Jerusalem (See Gal 4:21–31; Heb 12:18–29; Rev 21).[8] The true people of God are people whose citizenship is in heaven, a heavenly Jerusalem (Gal 4:27; Heb 12:22; Rev 21). The nation of Israel is an earthly people, now like all other peoples, concluded under sin. The people of God are those who in all times have been objects

8. It can be argued that Christ is the true Israel, to which all believing Jews and Gentiles are connected but that is beyond the scope of our purposes here.

of God's grace and the sanctifying work of Christ that saves from sin.[9] The saved are brought out of all those nations of this world, including Israel, to be in Christ where their true identity is no more Jew or Greek.

The argument that the New Testament church is Israel comes from a controversial reading of one single text, a reading that is then read into other passages. Paul said, "And as many as walk according to this rule, peace be on them, and mercy, and upon the Israel of God" (Gal 6:16). Fearing a misunderstanding that this verse is positing two different peoples of God, the argument is made that the word "and" (*kai*) should instead be translated as "even"—"*even* upon the Israel of God." In that reading, Paul would only be addressing one group of people, and the phrase "Israel of God" would only be another way of saying "those who walk by this rule." It would then be concluded that the New Testament church is called "Israel." While the translation of *kai* as "even" is within the semantic range of that word, the most overwhelming use of *kai* is as a conjunction. An appositive reading of that word (i.e., using it to mark a term being repeated in a different way) would require something in the context or syntax of the sentence to merit it being something other than a simple conjunction ("and").

The overall context of Galatians is a rebuke to the Judaizing teachers in the churches of Galatia, who were teaching that gentile converts could not be properly sanctified unless they forsook their ethnic customs and became Jewish proselytes. In the false belief of the Judaizers, being ethnic gentiles (whatever brand that may be) made them constantly unclean. They were considered unclean because they were not set apart by circumcision and because they did not follow the cleanliness laws of Moses in diet, dress, and other cultural distinctives. For some of the Jewish believers, until the gentiles forsook their ethnicity there could be no table fellowship between Jew and gentile. Paul argued that such was a false gospel and to be rejected. In the end and in the immediate context, Paul concludes that there is no advantage to those racial and cultural markers, "for in Christ Jesus neither circumcision availeth any thing, nor uncircumcision, but a new creature"

9. Note that contrary to dispensationalism, which says God still has a special relationship with the natural nation of Israel (or similar rhetoric that says the church is the "true" Israel), the elect transcend those earthly categories. The people of God are neither Jew nor gentile. It may have been to the Jew first but it went to the whole world. The Son of David may have begun with a limited reign in a limited space of time but ends with something far greater: a kingdom that has no end. Abraham was promised a tiny strip of land for a temporary people but the whole world was the end of that promise (Rom 4:9–13). And that greater reality comes in Christ.

(Gal 6:15). Neither Jew nor gentile is advantaged in any way. Their common advantage comes from being made new creations through Christ.

It is this common unity of the church as a new creation that leads to the prayer of Paul that "to as many as walk by that rule of faith, 'and' to the Israel of God, may peace and mercy be on both" (my own loose translation). The meaning of the prayer is that the believing gentiles and the believing Jews (the true Israelites as opposed to the unbelieving) may have peace and mercy from God together. It mirrors the teaching of the second chapter of the Letter to the Ephesians in which God made both Jew and gentile one, so making peace (Eph 2:14–16). It is a fitting prayer to end Paul's argument to the Galatian churches in rejection to the racial animus being promoted by the Judaizing influences. This single text does not stand as a prooftext for "replacement theology" and any type of racial animus that may result from such a doctrine. Instead, it promotes true unity between believing members of separate "races" in the church. We are all true sons of Abraham by faith in Christ and need not take on the earthly name of Israel to state that.

Realism easily falls into the same Judaizing folly. It advocates for disunity between races. Realism seeks to justify its "natural law" arguments with scriptural proofs as well. A favorite prooftext used by realists is Paul's word to Titus: "One of [them, a Cretan], even a prophet of their own, said, The Cretans are always liars, evil beasts, slow bellies" (Titus 1:12). For realism, this text seems to be the new John 3:16 due to its repeated use in their argumentation. They believe falsely that such a text:

A. Establishes that distinct races have their own "natural" moral deficiencies;

B. Shows that those moral deficiencies flow from their biology;

C. And shows that those moral deficiencies make it harder, if not impossible, to be as sanctified as other races.

While cultures may exhibit differing behavior due to embracing sin or righteousness in their public life, this is still a great leap of logic. A dishonest culture is not more morally lost than a sexually perverted one, nor is there any reason to believe that either result from a biologically determined racial source. The Cretans were not liars because they are Cretans but because they degraded their own culture over time. Just as any individual (regardless of race) may develop harmful habits, so may a society at large. The evil things that are now accepted in our current culture may suffice as an example. In a fallen world, comparing cultures is always comparing sinful cultures. Yes, I would rather not live in a culture that practices cannibalism, but while I say those words, I do not live in a sinless culture myself. Down the road there are people who look like me that just sexually assaulted a two-year-old to death and another woman who sold her toddler for sex to get methamphetamine. I can speak of cultural superiority in the abstract all day long, but sooner or later it must account for what is actually happening with "my own people."

To the last point (point C above), Paul did not believe that such a statement about the Cretans was speaking of anything more than acquired cultural idiosyncrasies. One would have to already believe in racial determinism (as realists assert in point B) to read racial determinism into Paul's text. That is the logical fallacy of affirming the consequent (i.e., assuming to be true what one wishes to prove). Paul also did not believe that such a moral observation hindered the ability of God to sanctify any of them. Paul tells Titus, "This witness is true. Wherefore, rebuke them sharply, that they may be sound in the faith" (Titus 1:13). The Cretans were not to be separated from but taught and corrected that they might be sound or healthy, functioning in the body of Christ as all others can and do.[10] Gospel ministry is sufficient to wash, justify, and sanctify any sin and any sinner (1 Cor 6:11).

The nature of realist arguments tends toward a belief that racial integration is an impediment to the spiritual growth of the church. They would say that just as nations thrive because of physical similarity, so does the church. Such is neither the doctrinal disposition of the Scriptures nor the historical New Testament reality in the church. Ethnic Jews and gentiles in one body was the glorious scandal of the New Testament, and its denial was labeled a false gospel. One of many examples is the mission work of the church of Antioch that resulted in Paul taking the gospel to the whole known world. Paul's ministry flourished from the sanctifying and prayerful work of Antiochian elders, an eldership that included Simon who was called Niger, meaning "black" (Acts 13:1–2). God brought a world-changing work out of a set of men that differed in skin color and likely class. They acted as one body ministering and the effects of that ministry are still felt.

10. Note: This point was recently a feature of a debate between New Testament scholar James White and a popular realist. When asked whether the Cretans could be sound in the faith, the realist refused to answer; White and Mahlet, "James White and Corey Mahlet Debate."

In fact, physical similarity is not only an unnecessary component to the sanctifying work of the Holy Spirit, but a possible impediment to it. If one holds one's father, mother, and brethren above their allegiance to Christ they affect their ability to follow Christ as they should (Matt 10:35–37). We too often lack wisdom to know what the proper points of our identity are due to our tendency to walk by sight instead of faith. It is not flesh and blood that enters the kingdom of God (1 Cor 15:50). It is only those that are born anew that enter (John 3:3, 5). It is in the kingdom of God that we multiply our brothers, and sisters, and mothers, and fathers (Matt 10:29–30). This of course is after the pattern of Christ, who, while His mother and brethren stood outside without Him, stretched out His hands to His followers and said that they were His mothers, brethren, and sisters; those who do the will of the Father (Matt 12:48–50). While we may earnestly desire those that are like us according to the flesh to be a part of that, the greater reality is found in faith and not in sight.

Racial pride is among those things that we are called upon to set aside for our sanctification. Paul argued from his racial distinctives as such:

> Though I might also have confidence in the flesh. If any other man thinketh that he hath whereof he might trust in the flesh, I more: Circumcised the eighth day, of the stock of Israel, of the tribe of Benjamin, an Hebrew of the Hebrews; as touching the law, a Pharisee. (Phil 3:4–5)

He was among those natural branches unaware that those branches in and of themselves were cut off from the covenants of Christ. He had things that a fleshly man might boast of when it came to his pedigree. However, what did he conclude in the light of Christ?

> But what things were gain to me, those I counted loss for Christ. Yea doubtless, and I count all things but loss for the excellency of the knowledge of Christ Jesus my Lord: for whom I have suffered the loss of all things, and do count them but dung, that I may win Christ, And be found in him, not having mine own righteousness, which is of the law, but that which is through the faith of Christ, the righteousness which is of God by faith: That I may know him, and the power of his resurrection, and the fellowship of his sufferings, being made conformable unto his death; If by any means I might attain unto the resurrection of the dead. (Phil 3:7–10)

Where are the realists, where are the Kinists, that speak that way about their flesh? Paul held all those things that boasted of racial and cultural pride as nothing, as dung, because what was to be had in Christ was greater and more worthy of his pursuit. May we in our sojourn in this world do the same.

CHAPTER 9

The People Christ Will Save

"And they sung a new song, saying, Thou art worthy to take the book, and to open the seals thereof: for thou wast slain, and hast redeemed us to God by thy blood out of every kindred, and tongue, and people, and nation; And hast made us unto our God kings and priests: and we shall reign on the earth."
REVELATION 5:9–10

"After this I beheld, and, lo, a great multitude, which no man could number, of all nations, and kindreds, and people, and tongues, stood before the throne, and before the Lamb, clothed with white robes, and palms in their hands; And cried with a loud voice, saying, Salvation to our God which sitteth upon the throne, and unto the Lamb." REVELATION 7:9–10

THE GREAT HOPE IS that true justice will be meted out in the end. Those that hold a faulty constructionist view of race tend to doubt the eschatological hope of the Christian and demand that "racial" justice (whatever that happens to mean) be meted out here and now. Much blood has been and will yet be spilled and lives ruined unjustly in pursuit of evening all scales to produce an elusive utopia with perfect equality. Driven by a covetous desire from sinful hearts operating in a sin-cursed world, true unity and equality will never be attained. The political folly of such is beyond the capacity of these brief observations to correct. It must only be said that such madness turns our eyes away from the greater hope of the coming kingdom of God. It is to that truth that we must now turn our gaze.

Letting political zeal ebb and flow after such impossible nonsense such as justice being perfected in a fallen world by sinful men will soon turn into flotsam and jetsam. Those that know Christ alone have a foretaste of the powers of that world to come. Those that do not know the Lord may sneak into churches unaware, trying to divide the church into so many various interest groups, and may lead many astray with their attempts to synthesize Christianity and Marxism or some kind of Kinistic national socialism. However, the Table of Christ is that sole place where all classes and races of men are leveled. Both Jew and Greek, both slave and freeman, both male and female, both rich and poor find communion together with Christ, baptized into one body, and vitally connected one to another in true unity. In fellowship at the Table of Christ, all are partakers of the promise that one day they will eat it as new with Him when He comes again (Matt 26:29).

Such a foretaste of heaven is lost on those who view all things with fleshly eyes. The believer sees in every fellow believer a brother, a fellow citizen of heaven, and one beloved of their Father. In our church fellowship, we are among those translated or changed together into a new people and nation, people born into the kingdom of the Son. For now, as long as we are tied to this world, we see that there are national and cultural differences. Nevertheless, the eyes of faith look beyond those to the day where even those differences are swallowed up into a greater reality. Flesh and blood will not inherit the kingdom of God (1 Cor 15:50). That truth cannot be uttered often enough. This matter of faith allows us to prefer the people of God over the vanities of our Adamic relations and find here and now a greater fulfillment therein. Christ has set us at variance with those of our own household, as accounted by the flesh, while we pursue Him (Matt 10:34–39).

There is a greater equality in glorification yet to be that the present Table of our Lord is but a foretaste. I do not mean that our future glory will be sameness of reward for the faithful. In the end, some will have thirtyfold and some a hundredfold. It is not now readily apparent that we know who deserves what. That lies in the wisdom of God's judgment of us who will Himself delight in making those who appear last first and those who appear first last. I also do not mean that there will be loss of all individuality. We will indeed be known and we as individuals will differ as one star differs from another star in glory (1 Cor 15:41). We will sit with Abraham and Isaac, and we will know them as Abraham and Isaac (Matt 8:11). In that sense, something of our history will be carried into the world yet to come.

However, that history will be seen as a redeemed history. We will sing that we have been loosed (or washed, depending on the manuscript tradition) from our sins by the one that loved us (Rev 1:5–6). We will cease to share in the corruptible, the weak, the perishable things of this world and share in the incorruptible things of Christ. Our works for Christ follow us there and make us distinct. Likeness to Christ gives the parameters to our glory (1 John 3:2). "Adam's likeness now efface, Stamp Thine image in its place."[1]

There are those that make a lot of noise about flesh and blood in the here and now, and they imagine, without scriptural warrant, that those distinctions will be prominent yet in eternity. This fiction is foisted upon scriptural eschatology. It is not worth mentioning race-based ideas of redemption here. Fools may believe that the color of one's skin or national origin make them solely redeemed among men, or at least more redeemed than others. Such folly did not come from the pages of Scripture, rather it came from their own false fancies. I would rather challenge here an argument purported by many realists that is too easily adopted by those who do not hold their hurtful conclusions. Having already set aside the present reality (i.e., that the redeemed of the Lord are neither Jew nor gentile), they will argue that in eternity we will yet maintain the biologically "racial" identity that we had on earth. They argue that around the throne of God there is going to be *every nation, tribe, and tongue*. Therefore, they argue that racial distinction is maintained even in heaven.

The argument can be summed up by sentiments expressed in a conversation with one I deem to be a fellow Christian (who stated to me that he abhorred realism). He stated, "Christ redeems people *in* their ethnicity, not *from* it. The Marriage Supper of the Lamb will be rich with flavor, language, and custom, all glorifying the risen Christ." I do not take issue with the general sentiment of these words, and I believe that this argument was made in good faith. However, realists use this kind of argument to combat the errors of constructionists, but they use it to press their error of racial permanency (i.e., race being an immutable reality). I take issue therefore only with the unspoken claim.

As I have repeatedly asserted, it is a mistake to see "flesh and blood" as inheritors of the kingdom of God (1 Cor 15:50). The sentiments of my brother above contradict that truth. The principle of the already/not yet fulfillment is pertinent here (i.e., the doctrine that some truths in Christ are both already partially fulfilled in this world and still wait for a broader

1. Wesley, "Hark! The Herald Angels Sing."

fulfillment in the world to come). We *were* gentiles, or we *were* Jews, but we *are not* those things anymore. Our present standing in Christ is our identity—though in this present evil world there is a connection to things according to the flesh. In our glorification, that will be a totally realized eschatology.

Consider what the biblical text does say and how it differs from a realist sentiment. John tells us that those around the throne of God praised the Lamb and the One that sat on the throne saying, "[You have] redeemed us to God by thy blood out of every kindred, and tongue, and people, and nation; And hast made us unto our God kings and priests: and we shall reign on the earth" (Rev 5:9–10). Note then a subtle and likely unintentional shift in syntax between the stance of my brother (speaking under influence of a realist argument) and the actual text. Realism contends that "Christ redeems people *in* their ethnicity, not *from* it." This shift brings forward a lot of racial assumptions. However, the text states explicitly that the redeemed of the Lord are redeemed *from* or *out of* the nations. The contention against realism then lies here in the syntax of the sentence. Both my brother and I can maintain that the nations will indeed flow into the new Jerusalem (Rev 21:26; Ps 100:1), but this syntax causes us to see our salvation (both in this world and in the world to come) differently.

The argument falls on a single Greek preposition and how it should be translated. The preposition *ek* in its normal usage implies separation from something—this is called an ablative meaning ("from" or "out of"). At the time of the writing of the New Testament, *ek* was becoming the chief means of expressing separation, whereas in classical Greek it was expressed in another way.[2] There are of course other possible meanings of this Greek preposition,[3] but its overwhelming use is to describe a separation. If in this context the preposition carries that idea, then the reading would be that those around the throne were peoples "brought out" of their former state to be a part of something else. Those who wish to translate the preposition as something other than "out of" would need to make a sound argument against its normal usage.

Going beyond semantics, there is contextual support for this reading being a description of those around the throne being brought *out of*

2. Classical Greek was more likely to use the genitive noun declension to express an ablative meaning.

3. Possible alternate uses of *ek* would include a description of the source of something, its cause, how something is part of something else, or the means by which something is done. See Wallace, *Greek Grammar Beyond the Basics*, 108, 371–72.

various nations to be part of something else. The text does not only contain the state *from which* they were separated but also the state *to which* they were translated. That is, they came out of different nations and instead were made kings and priests unto God. This upholds the spiritual reality we hold now by faith. We *were* gentiles but have been translated into the kingdom of Christ. Our citizenship *is* there already. Those around the throne make up one new people or holy *ethnos* after the pattern of the new creation. There will then be a unified "us" singing about what we once were and rejoicing in what we will (or at that point have) become. The same language is emphatic when it is repeated in the seventh chapter of Revelation as well.

Parallels in Scripture also confirm this reading. In the Septuagint (i.e., the Greek translation of the Old Testament used by the apostles), the same preposition is used of Abraham when God called him out of the other nations to make him one new nation (Gen 12:1–3). The fact that the greater children of the faith of Abraham will sing the same refrain in the end is a powerful argument for maintaining the normal use of the Greek preposition, as opposed to the realist interpretation. Abraham did not remain a Syrian by the grace of God. He was redeemed from it and so will all the people of God.

Everything that realism treasures in its "blood and soil" ideology is not what the redeemed of the Lord sings about around the throne. Their land will be the new heavens and earth, and their blood will be the blood of Christ alone which they will commonly share. Their borders are no longer the borders of this world. Despite whatever differences that they had in this world, they together inherit all things and share that same border. Sharing that same border as fellow heirs with Christ, they will also speak the same language. There will be a return to a pure language whereby with unity they will praise the Lord (Zeph 3:9). There will not be different languages in heaven but one, just as there will not be differing kingdom borders but one. Their culture will be the culture of the heavenly Jerusalem shaped by Christ Himself. All this will be shared as the unifying kingdom experience by all that will be glorified. There will be only the race of Christ, justified people made perfect.

The realist would have one believe that every individual in heaven will forever have the things they say constitute one's race here on earth (e.g., borders, language, culture, genetics, etc.). However, glorification will not be a desolate Babel; it will be Babel redeemed and not left under judgment. The church at Pentecost, where all heard the good words of God in their own tongue and glorified God together, was a foretaste of that greater reality. The church meeting in common citizenship in Christ now is the same foretaste of glory. The description of the glorified saints is a redeemed description emptied of all the curses of judgment. I will not bear the sins of my present culture there in all their vanity. I will be redeemed from them and so will all else who share that fate.

A total redemption is wrought for the saints by Christ. This redemption of the body is called an adoption by Paul, which further highlights the translation from one familial state to another (Rom 8:16–23). All that was in Adam will be effaced, and they will be alive only in Christ. The argument that the development of separate nations or races is a necessary consequence of the created nature of man has little room for a single kingdom under Christ in the end. That ideology would necessitate rather the insertion of continued and eternal division of the family of God. In the fall, mankind was in the vanity of rebelling nations and tribes. From one blood all the nations of men groped in darkness. Through the blood that redeemed them they will all be one people unto God, dwelling forever in the light of God's presence. Even now in our experience, the kingdom of God is not the customs of men like meat and drink, "but righteousness, and peace, and joy in the Holy Ghost" (Rom 14:17). In the end, there we will all eat at the table prepared by our one Father and will know the fullness of what this means: "Behold, the tabernacle of God is with men, and he will dwell with them, and they shall be his people, and God himself shall be with them, and be their God" (Rev 21:3).

CHAPTER 10

Defining My Neighbor

"And Jesus answered him, The first of all the commandments is, Hear, O Israel; The Lord our God is one Lord: And thou shalt love the Lord thy God with all thy heart, and with all thy soul, and with all thy mind, and with all thy strength: this is the first commandment. And the second is like, namely this, Thou shalt love thy neighbour as thyself. There is none other commandment greater than these. And the scribe said unto him, Well, Master, thou hast said the truth: for there is one God; and there is none other but he: And to love him with all the heart, and with all the understanding, and with all the soul, and with all the strength, and to love his neighbour as himself, is more than all whole burnt offerings and sacrifices. And when Jesus saw that he answered discreetly, he said unto him, Thou art not far from the kingdom of God." MARK 12:29–34

RHETORIC FROM CONSTRUCTIONISTS AND realists alike has sounded the clarion call for a reexamination of our scriptural command to love our neighbor. For the constructionist, the need to "even the scales" that appear to favor one group over the other drives them to despise the one perceived as favored. This results in a denial of any real claim to justice or need of mercy among that group. "Eat the rich" is a dividing cry. In traditional Marxist terms, the proletariat (i.e., the working class) can never act unjustly toward the bourgeoisie (i.e., the managing class). Such is the Marxist doctrine of inherent antagonism. The oppressed class is free to commit all types of violence against the favored group and the favored have no right to cry out for justice. Justice is whatever the oppressed decide to do according to its twisted liberation theology and its perverted concept of justice. To the constructionist, a neighbor must only be one of the "oppressed" class and never otherwise. The rhetoric of the realists and their insisting on an *ordo amoris* (i.e., "order of loves") as an applied political ideology is of no greater moral value. It slowly downgrades all who are not genetically similar from the status of a neighbor. Dissimilarity excuses them from a full consideration of mercy and justice contrary to the ones they consider as "near."

Regarding the realist concept of a neighbor, it is not that the *ordo amoris* concept has no bearing in our life. A man is to love his God supremely, and then his neighbor as himself secondarily. That is the only order that Moses, rather Christ, permitted when expounding the law. There are other biblical categories that are applicable—specific natural affections to attend to. One is to naturally love his wife as his own flesh, and parents are to naturally care for and nurture their children in ways that are neither proper nor advantageous to express otherwise. Children are to honor their parents. This demands more from them individually than any responsibility they have to people outside of that immediate context. The greater experience of love should be felt by those closest to its source. Early fathers who taught *ordo amoris* did so believing that such love was first directed toward God above all, flowed out to those of one's house, and then flowed outward as opportunity was had to express it. To use it for a reason to deny justice or shut up bowels of mercy toward another is far from that meaning.[1]

There is an aspect of this *ordo amoris* infected with contemporary thought. Carl Schmitt, a Nazi Party political philosopher, for example, has in recent years been resurrected in far-right politics. His resurrection is due to his expounding of the touted friend/enemy distinction that he presented as a governing political theory. Much like Marxist theories and the social Darwinist thought of his day, Schmitt placed conflict as a central element for group identity, and the recognition of threats to the group to be principal to *all* political decision-making. It is readily agreed that the duty of providing security to the populace necessitates recognizing potential threats to peace, but Schmitt offered this as a general principle for all governance. One needs little imagination to see how such a political theory

1. Admittedly, when speaking of the use of limited resources, principles to wisely use those resources to the greatest effect would include making a difference between those in greater or lesser need. This however is not a principle of governance which acts indifferently to the command to love. A government acting in love is a contemporary ideology. A government is to act justly, without respect of persons.

could lend itself to cruelty and injustice, especially when the lines between government and the private sector are blurred.

The difficulty in differentiating between the political and personal outworking of such a doctrine is our main concern here. As a political ideology, it ignores the multiple nuances that drive treaties and alliances between nations and peoples. As a personal policy, it runs contrary to scriptural imperatives. As one blurs their political views into all aspects of their life, it infects their moral behavior toward those they encounter. If one has already adopted a realist perspective on nature, seeing other races as a threat in the friend/enemy distinction further distorts that perspective. The *ordo amoris* and the friend/enemy distinction in practice is the outworking of loving only the one that is "near" to you (by which they only mean "similar to") and "hating" the enemy (by which they mean the one "not similar"). This very philosophy was contradicted by Christ who said that those who say "love your neighbor, but hate your enemy" are acting contrary to the righteousness of His law (Matt 5:43–48).

When *ordo amoris* is embraced as a cold calculus for who is and who is not worthy of charity or justice, it then is opposed to the greater Christian ethic. Such a cold calculus fits well into the miserly heart of fallen human nature, which needs little excuse to shut up its bowels of compassion. We tend to only love those that love us and to only give to those who are likely to return the favor. This is natural but not praiseworthy (Matt 5:46–47).

Scriptural imperatives, however, call on all to love those that God gives them to love.

> Owe no man any thing, but to love one another: for he that loveth another hath fulfilled the law. For this, Thou shalt not commit adultery, Thou shalt not kill, Thou shalt not steal, Thou shalt not bear false witness, Thou shalt not covet; and if there be any other commandment, it is briefly comprehended in this saying, namely, Thou shalt love thy neighbour as thyself. Love worketh no ill to his neighbour: therefore love is the fulfilling of the law. (Rom 13:8–10)

Paul here speaks of what we owe to men generally. There are three truths he sets forth. First, there is the summary of our true debt. "Owe no man anything, but to love one another." On the surface of this imperative, there is wisdom for our practical lives. We should avoid debts in our economy for such will engender bondage (Prov 22:7). However, this goes much deeper than a lesson on proper budgeting. It is in the context of our civil duties toward the powers over us and speaks of our need to pay to all what is due to them. Generally, to society we are already indebted. This debt knows no racial or class-based boundaries (Rom 1:14). The debt of love is that debt for which we have no discharge and can ethically afford no default.

Then there is the deeper matter of the love we owe. When Christ expressed a legitimate reason for exemption from a certain levied tax, He gave Peter provision to pay and stated to pay without complaint, "lest we should offend them" (Matt 17:27). Our external compliance even with unjust laws is a vehicle for us to express the righteous love of Christ. A bruised reed He would not break. If we offend in our politics, we place potential obstacles before men and we potentially make the gospel of Christ an obnoxious thing. Paul had already spoken of our debt to all in the first chapter of Romans and how that was to the end of preaching the gospel (Rom 1:14–15). Sharing the gospel without offense or occasions of offense is the greatest act of love toward our fellow men. In an age where the most sinful acts are politically enmeshed, this becomes increasingly difficult—for we must preach the whole counsel of God.

Wrangling over political parties, laws, taxes, political personalities, and such has little to do with our ethical honesty and stance against sin. Those tend to put walls up between men and Christ and ought to be avoided. The true debt is love for all who God has placed before us and not allegiance to things that are not of the kingdom of Christ. Let it never be said of us that we were all about winning people to our political persuasion or cause instead of winning them to Christ. Let it never be said that our civil behavior made our witness stink in the nostrils of those who beheld our life.

Going beyond the summary of our duty, the true source of our debt is brought forth: "For he that loveth another hath fulfilled the law." There is a greater debt to God and His law that ought to consume us. Our love toward others is our devotion to God. We cannot be obedient to God without giving ourselves in love to others. Paul here is denying wholesale the doctrine of antinomianism (i.e., lawlessness). Christ's righteousness in the law is fulfilled in us (Rom 8:4). And we are to walk in His righteousness (2 Cor 5:21; Rom 6:1–4). Those who turn Christianity into a license to fulfill selfish lusts are enemies of the gospel of Christ (Jude 1:4; Phil 3:19). On the other hand, Christianity is not reduced to compliance to commands, a list of things not to do. One is not righteous if the command is simply externally kept. Thus, Paul continues:

> For this, Thou shalt not commit adultery, Thou shalt not kill, Thou shalt not steal, Thou shalt not bear false witness, Thou shalt not covet; and if there be any other commandment, it is briefly comprehended in this saying, namely, Thou shalt love thy neighbour as thyself. (Rom 13:9)

All the prohibitions of the Scriptures toward our fellow man are summed up in one grand positive command (Matt 22:35–40). Therefore, Paul also denies legalism. Legalism focuses on a list of prohibitions and external forms of religious activity, and it proclaims that those things fulfill our obligation. The things they ought to do, the greater part to be done, includes the acts of mercy (Matt 23:23). There is no encouragement to ignore the small things, but to focus on them only as they relate to the greater principle. God would have mercy and not sacrifice (Matt 9:13; 12:7). God would have us care for others and not just keep ourselves from killing them or robbing them. One is not living righteously by obeying the former without the latter. To not commit murder or adultery, to keep yourself from covetousness and to not steal, is not the sum of righteousness. The sum is what the good Samaritan did. That was the righteousness of Christ.

In case Paul missed any, he said if there are any other commands that are like those so named in the summary, include them under one single heading too. All those commands are directives to love. To not commit adultery is to love faithfulness to one's wife and all who are blessed by that testimony. To not kill is to love, encourage, and speak blessings on your brother or to the stranger. To not steal is to love and give that which God has given us to those He brings to us. To not covet is to esteem others better than yourself.

Through Christ, we comprehend the real sum of the law. Every prohibitive command implies its opposite character, which is kept only through love. Paul says elsewhere:

> For, brethren, ye have been called unto liberty; only use not liberty for an occasion to the flesh, but by love serve one another. For all the law is fulfilled in one word, even in this; Thou shalt love thy neighbour as thyself. (Gal 5:13–14)

This is the royal law by which one can say they have done well only when it is done (Jas 2:8). The obligation will never come to an end in this fallen world. This debt to God will always be ours. It is owed not just in sentiments but in deeds, and not only in deeds but in words. It encompasses all we say, do, and think toward any that God sets before us. He that gives to the poor lends to the Lord (Prov 19:17). As we do to the least, we do it to Him (Matt 25:45).

The testimony of our true debt when paid is brought out. "Love worketh no ill to his neighbor: therefore love is the fulfilling of the law." Matthew Henry stated, "Love is a living, active principle of obedience to the whole law."[2] One can speak of the virtues of hatred and violence in the spiritual sense (i.e., hatred of sin, warfare against God's enemies), but such virtues are never said to be the fulfilling of God's law. In this matter of civil society, love alone demonstrates to the world the perfect righteousness of Christ. It gives testimony to the gospel lived out. Amid the sinful race of Adam, and its several sinful races, it is the resurrection or regeneration that works love through Christ. Love works no ill. It does no harm. Like their Lord, the follower of Christ breaks no bruised reeds in their tender compassion for their neighbor. The love of Christ lived does away with the need for constraint from law. Sinful selfishness of men necessitates the growth of government to contain those passions (Prov 29:2). Christian morality exhibits a freedom that can only be found in the gospel lived out. If men walk contrary to the law in the lost state of sinfulness, then they will lie, cheat, steal, rape, murder, and do all things so they can fulfill their lust. When men know the love of Christ, they uncover springs of love toward men. The laws of men exist to curb the lust of men; the gospel replaces lust with love. "And hope maketh not ashamed; because the love of God is shed abroad in our hearts by the Holy Ghost which is given unto us" (Rom 5:5). The concept of Christian charity, the acts of love, sum up this fulfilling:

> Charity suffereth long, and is kind; charity envieth not; charity vaunteth not itself, is not puffed up, Doth not behave itself unseemly, seeketh not her own, is not easily provoked, thinketh no evil; Rejoiceth not in iniquity, but rejoiceth in the truth; Beareth all things, believeth all things, hopeth all things, endureth all things. Charity never faileth. (1 Cor 13:4–8)

Coming back to the story of the good Samaritan, this matter of animus against our fellow man is answered in relation to this very law of love. This law of love is among the holiness codes that contained those very abominable acts for which God destroyed nations over. It is the law that Christ said is second only to man's duty to love God wholly. Christ said to the man that wished to justify himself, "This do, and thou shalt live" (Luke 10:25–29). Neither the realist nor the constructionist is able from

2. Henry, *Matthew Henry's Commentary* 6:13.

their framework to speak in such a manner. In the same spirit, the one attempting to justify himself before Christ desired to limit this command in some way. "Who is my neighbor?" How this is answered reveals our heart. Is it answered via the friend/enemy distinction? Is it calculated with the *ordo amoris*? Is it answered with preference to kinship? Is it answered by principles of likeness? Is it answered with the paradigm of favored versus oppressed conflict?

In the commandment, the term "neighbor" (*plésion*) is an adverb being used as a noun. As an adverb it means "near" and as a noun it means "the near one." The way Christ applied the teaching sets the term "neighbor" outside of any correlation to *ordo amoris* or class identity. It is not a nearness of relationship, ethnicity, or class that Christ speaks of as an example of the fulfillment of this law. The Samaritan was near in the sense of circumstantial nearness and not familial or ethnic nearness. The circumstance of being able to meet a need and being confronted with one that had the need is the circumstance in which one is to love his neighbor—without any other qualifier. The Samaritan had a means of treating the wounds of the dying Jew and did, where others failed to do so who met other criteria for nearness. The Samaritan also had the means of carrying that same Jew to safety and providing space for recovery. The fact that there was ethnic and tribal hatred between Jews and Samaritans did not excuse the Samaritan from the obligation of love. The other two that failed to love were under that same law, but they transgressed it.

James handled this same law as it related to distinctions of class.

> My brethren, have not the faith of our Lord Jesus Christ, the Lord of glory, with respect of persons. For if there come unto your assembly a man with a gold ring, in goodly apparel, and there come in also a poor man in vile raiment; And ye have respect to him that weareth the gay clothing, and say unto him, Sit thou here in a good place; and say to the poor, Stand thou there, or sit here under my footstool: Are ye not then partial in yourselves, and are become judges of evil thoughts? (Jas 2:1–3)

Christ taught His disciples to love those who cannot advantage them. The argument to those who claim *ordo amoris* or the friend/enemy distinction is that we ought to love those who are closest to us, for that is for our advantage and the advantage of our lineage and heritage. The constructionist applies the same principle to class. The advantage/disadvantage dichotomy is not the application that James made. The love of the Christian is not that which is acted on to reap some later benefit for oneself or for one's own. To show this, James goes to the law of love as a schoolmaster.

> If ye fulfil the royal law according to the scripture, Thou shalt love thy neighbour as thyself, ye do well: But if ye have respect to persons, ye commit sin, and are convinced of the law as transgressors. For whosoever shall keep the whole law, and yet offend in one point, he is guilty of all. For he that said, Do not commit adultery, said also, Do not kill. Now if thou commit no adultery, yet if thou kill, thou art become a transgressor of the law. (Jas 2:8–11)

There are three distinct truths in this portion of the Scriptures. The first truth is that the law gives a perfect standard of righteousness that excludes injustice (and, on the contrary, demands charity). James stated, "If ye fulfill the royal law according to the scripture, Thou shalt love thy neighbor as thyself, ye do well." This "if" speaks of the conditional application of the law by any given individual. The word of God always practically meets us in the circumstances of life. It is not a dry, academic voice but a living voice that speaks into our daily activities. Some of James' readers had fallen into a pharisaical trap, having begun to see themselves as worthy individuals and as being among other worthy ones. For our purposes, we may apply it to some who see their culture as more worthy than the seeming poverty produced by others—being among a better class, with a better history, and a possibly better future. James' words are the language of the law confronting both them and us.

Again, this is the royal law of the Supreme Sovereign speaking into the realm of our practical experience. We are not higher than this edict, whatever we may think ourselves and our heritage to be. It demands something toward all men at all possible times where it may be practiced—in word or deed. This is the standard of excellence. This is how we honor our King among His subjects. This is the law, like the law of the Medes, which cannot be altered. This is the royal edict of mercy from our King to all, and we are to be its faithful heralds and practitioners. We are ambassadors of the Lawgiver, and we perform our duties by this great law. This royal law is the measure by which all subjects are judged. "I counsel thee to keep the king's commandment. . . . Where the word of a king is, there is power" (Eccl 8:2, 4). This is jurisdictional truth. It is in harmony with the whole of the Scriptures. Moses wrote, "Thou shalt love thy neighbor as thyself: I am the LORD" (Lev 19:18). James said that if you do this, if you continue in doing this, you do well. This is reminiscent of the rebuke of Cain: "If thou doest well, shalt thou not be accepted? and if thou doest not well, sin lieth at the door" (Gen 4:7). Or, as Solomon said about the commandment of the king, "Whoso keepeth the commandment shall feel no evil thing" (Eccl 8:5). This is the expression of your righteousness, and it, as we soon shall see, is filthy rags.

Can any fulfill this on their own? James' readers saw themselves as fulfillers of the Lord's commands, as they had set themselves up as judges over the worthiness of their fellow men. Now, behold the law! This is what the one true Lawgiver has said to you. Having taught the law, do you now break the law (Rom 2:17–20)? Is this solid ground for any to rest upon? Or will you prove to be forgetful hearers of the law and not true doers, as James already warned some in his first chapter? If one is a fulfiller of the law, it will be in this: "For all the law is fulfilled in one word, *even* in this; Thou shalt love thy neighbor as thyself" (Gal 5:14). The meaning of the term "neighbor" included both the rich and the poor that are highlighted here (the poor which they despised), as before it included both Jew and Samaritan.

James pressed forward to note the act of injustice that convicts us as sinners under the law. "But if ye have respect to persons, ye commit sin, and are convinced of the law as transgressors." You do well in the eyes of the law, if you keep to it. If you love your neighbor perfectly you have nothing to fear. However, there is a problem. The perfection of the law is conditional. James said "if" you have respect for persons, that law convicts you to be a transgressor. Injustice reveals the work of sin. In the first verse, James said to have respect for persons is contrary to the faith of our Lord Jesus Christ, whom James called the Lord of glory. Now it is contrary also to the law itself. Therefore, it breaks the greatest and the second greatest commandment. To not love your neighbor is to not love your King that so commanded you. The word "convinced" (or "convict") is literally "to be exposed as." You are caught red-handed, without an excuse, as one breaking and despising the King's laws. It is written with large letters over you, "Transgressor!"

The law stands now as the irrefutable prosecutor and judge. It lays the evidence of our crime out and makes even our own hearts cry out, "Guilty!" It exposes us to be in truth workers of iniquity—another word for injustice (Matt 7:23). Everyone before us is our neighbor, but respecting only some of them as opposed to others denies that truth. The one in need of our mercy is specifically the one we are obligated to love. The law of love is destroyed when one gives mercy only to some, those they hope to be advantaged thereby. We are the priest and the Levite passing on the other side of the road in this instance. The law possesses the power of conviction. You have crossed the line into unrighteousness by failing to care about the one that is before you. All your perceived signs of righteousness are now meaningless. Paul in agreement said, "If thou be a breaker of the law, thy circumcision is made uncircumcision" (Rom 2:25). Or, as Isaiah said, "All our righteousness is filthy rags" (Isa 64:6).

James clearly states that the guilt that is incurred is total and declares us to be completely lawless. We are exposed by the law as lawbreakers and not just the law about loving our neighbor. The whole of the law condemns us. "For whosoever shall keep the whole law, and yet offend in one point, he is guilty of all." It could be expressed like this: the one to whom the law has been given is obligated to keep it wholly. Ellicott stated, "As a chain is snapped by failure of the weakest link, so the whole Law, in its harmony and completeness as beheld by God, is broken by one offence. . . . The penalty falls, of its own natural weight and incidence, on the culprit."[3] There is not just an irrefutable guilt, but an irredeemable guilt that is carried. We cannot now seek refuge in another point of the law and say we are still good. The whole law condemns us. We have not loved our neighbor and every law that defines what that means has been uniformly breached.

Our Lord's brother further elaborated, "For he that said, Do not commit adultery, said also, Do not kill. Now if thou commit no adultery, yet if thou kill, thou art become a transgressor of the law." These two commands were more closely defined by our Lord, the content specifically of the Sermon on the Mount being a point of dependence for James. To look on a woman with lust is to commit adultery, and to despise one's brother in your heart is to commit murder (Matt 5:21–27). Here, James summarizes the second table of the law where those commands are found. They are violations of our neighbor, the opposite of love. One may not have violated his neighbor's wife but, as defined by Christ, if one has demeaned the character of another, they are still guilty. The same Lord gave each command, and we bow in equal guilt of treason against Him as those that break His law. Not all may legitimately be called adulterers, but all can be legitimately called transgressors. James invokes the same principle as Ezekiel: "When I shall say to the righteous, that he shall surely live; if he trust to his own righteousness, and commit iniquity, all his righteousnesses shall not be remembered; but for his iniquity that he hath committed, he shall die for it" (Ezek 33:13).

3. Ellicott, "James 2."

No one can simply rest in the law. This does not mean that all sin is equal. Judas had a greater sin than Pilate (John 19:11), it would be more tolerable for some in the judgment (Matt 10:15), and some sin against a greater light (Luke 12:47). However, all who break the law belong to the same class. To walk safely over a precipice a great distance and then to stumble one step short of the end is still to fall headlong to destruction. If you have kept yourself from adultery but still commit murder, you still have broken the Ten Commandments; you are still guilty of breaking the whole of God's law. Paul later stated, "For as many as are of the works of the law are under the curse: for it is written, Cursed is every one that continueth not in all things which are written in the book of the law to do them" (Gal 3:10).

The letter of James reminds us of our guilt in our relationship between injustice and the gospel.

> So speak ye, and so do, as they that shall be judged by the law of liberty. For he shall have judgment without mercy, that hath shewed no mercy; and mercy rejoiceth against judgment. (Jas 2:12–13)

James would have us speak clearly of our guilt before the law, for such becomes one that is judged by the higher rule of the gospel. This is the language of David in his repentance: "Against thee [God], thee only, have I sinned, and done this evil in thy sight: that thou mightest be justified when thou speakest, and be clear when thou judgest" (Ps 51:4). James would have us not only speak openly of our guilt but to do the law in the same spirit. The phrase "law of liberty" was introduced by James in his first chapter (Jas 1:25). The law of liberty is the law of the Spirit of life in Christ Jesus (Rom 8:2–3), expressing the will of God in our regeneration (Jas 1:18), that word that is alone able to save us (Jas 1:21), and that law into which we look into and continue in as true disciples. It is the fullness of our faith in Christ, the Lord of Glory (Jas 2:1). The gospel teaches us to walk in liberty as disciples of Christ (John 8:31, 32, 36). It becomes all who believe the gospel to walk in repentance and in newness of life, free from the former chains of their sin (Rom 6). One speaking by the spirit of repentance does no evil to his neighbor. This ultimately in James' letter prepares the reader for a more important conversation about having works and faith, not just wishing well but doing well (Jas 2:14–17). Living under the law of liberty, that is, living under gospel truth, directs us to true love of God and our neighbor.

The phrase "law of liberty" calls the reader to focus back on the reality of their faith in Christ. He is our life—the standard of our life. We shall all stand before His judgment seat (Rom 14:10). Our conformity to His truth as our Lord will be the substance of that judgment. The law was a means of seeing that character we were supposed to put on. The judgment is the Son's (John 5:27). The gospel of the kingdom, the law of liberty, the royal law, the reign of grace are all synonymous for this new rule of life from which we live, which governs our speaking and doing (Matt 24:14; Rom 5:21). Yes, the believer is not under the law, but under grace (Rom 6:14). Under grace we are taught to live in the righteousness of Christ (2 Cor 5:21; Gal 2:20; Titus 2:11–12).

We will conclude with James' warning and encouragement: "For he shall have judgment without mercy, that hath shewed no mercy; and mercy rejoiceth against judgment." There is much from the Sermon on the Mount here. At the very least, these words declare that the measure that we show mercy will be the measure that we will find mercy under the law of liberty. It mirrors the teaching of Christ about the exercise of forgiveness and our experience of the same (Matt 6:14–15). There are two possibilities for the disciple of Christ. Either they will be subject to the same measure of merciless judgment that they give to others—what measure we measure will be measured to us again (Matt 7:1–5)—or they will live a life of merciful practice that rejoices against all judgment against them. God will show mercy to those who are merciful (Ps 18:25–26). If any man will shut his ears to the cry of the poor, he also will cry without being heard (Prov 21:13). "The merciful man doeth good to his own soul: but he that is cruel troubleth his own flesh" (Prov 11:13). However, to the merciful they shall receive mercy (Matt 5:7). When justice demands payment from the merciful man, mercy stands exalted and turns justice's demand away.

One may question what this warning says about the nature of the one that shows no mercy. Are they true disciples or not? The continued context of James is to differentiate the true disciple from the hearer only (between a dead and living faith)—a theme introduced in his first chapter. Therefore, judgment without mercy can be declared without dilution, without wrestling with the idea of it being fully experienced by the true disciple. This text is meant to warn false brethren who are not showing themselves to be children of the Father (Matt 5:43–48).

Yet this warning is not without teeth for the true disciple. We can still speak of our God's frown upon us in our temporal experience, in His corrections of us. It would be hard to describe the true disciple as being without mercy (Heb 12:11). This seems far more descriptive of the rich man being denied the drop of water and the cursed being sent away into everlasting fire

(Luke 16:24–26; Matt 25:41, 46). Meyer stated, "That which in the judgment passes sentence on Christians, who shall be judged [by the law of liberty], is thus mercy. Against the unmerciful the judgment will be unmerciful."[4] Mercy rejoicing or boasting here is meant to show the disposition of God toward the true believer, the one conformed to the Son's righteous image. He rejoices in God's mercy for God is merciful (Luke 18:13–14). Our judgment is through the law of liberty that is declared by the gospel of our Lord. It rejoices against all judgment against us. It induces us to live according to mercy, and those who are otherwise will be judged (Rom 1:31). The gospel thus induces us and leads us into this rejoicing mercy.

4. Meyer, "James 2."

APPENDIX

Forgiveness

"FORGIVING ONE ANOTHER EVEN AS CHRIST HATH FORGIVEN YOU." EPHESIANS 4:32

INEVITABLY THE TOPIC OF race in a fallen world is related to animosity from offenses both real and imagined. The lucrative business of media thrives on creating conflict and as such one cannot partake in media without exposing themselves to that conflict. Our eyes affect our hearts. We are regularly shown people who look like us being hurt and even killed by those who do not look like us. Whether it reflects a true or a distorted reality, that propaganda works hatred in our heart and easily becomes generalized beyond the limits of the individual story. In the first chapter, I spoke of a representative of a Christian Identity cult that urged me, saying, "Don't you see what is happening to your people?" Such urging is effective because it seems to fit what we see (or rather, what we are presented). To this person's point, where are we "seeing" these things? We are beholding them daily through our media sources and rarely with our direct sight. These images deepen how we interpret any friend/enemy distinction as we see ourselves in those that look like us and enemies in the ones that hurt them. Just as people appropriate the achievements of people who "look like them," they are just as liable with or without cause to take up the offenses of the same. Further, with or without any personal injury to themselves, they will respond with malice and hatred against those that they perceive as their oppressors.

There are times that there are real injuries, not just generalized ones. This creates a real pull for that to turn into generalized hatred and malice.

The prince of this world is tempting us to take up a spirit of revenge and bitterness. The temptation is for us to forsake the mercy of the gospel for unforgiving malice against those who seem to be our enemies.

Forgiveness is central to the practice of mercy. One of the greatest apologetics for the truth of the Christian faith is found in its practice. There is a common recognition that there is a greater reality to forgiveness than is found in human nature alone. "To err is human, but to forgive is divine." Therefore, forgiveness is a Christian expression, given that it alone is an incarnational faith. There is little room for forgiveness outside of Christianity, but there is a broadness for it within the Christian faith.

In secular thought, forgiveness as taught in the Scriptures is a weakness in nature. Darwinism is about survival of the fittest. Therefore, forgiveness in evolutionary terms must be weighed against that which aids in the survival of the group or species. For an individual or society to allow themselves to be defrauded without retribution runs contrary to nature. Nevertheless, that is how forgiveness is seen when practiced biblically. In the faulty wisdom of this world, such a thought would guarantee the weakness and eventual death of those who practice it.

This contradiction does not negate the need for naturalists to explain mercy as a phenomenon. Darwinism may say that sympathy arose for the survival of humanity, and that sympathy may cause one to have mercy when it is somehow advantageous. On the side of the injured party, there may be a desire to receive mercy when revenge is pointed toward them. However, what reason would the injured party have, who have power to exact revenge, to extend forgiveness when there is no apparent advantage in it? This is where the discussion of mercy becomes meaningful. If they extended mercy, how would that help their survival? If they showed some semblance of mercy, it must (in the evolutionary view) help the forgiving party. Nevertheless, if that is the case, what they end up with is not forgiveness at all. They end up with a form of mercy that is only extended if it is advantageous. Naturalism destroys mercy.

Mercy as taught in the Scriptures is of a different nature altogether. In the first place, forgiveness is a matter of justice. To have forgiveness, you must have an injured party. In the eyes of justice, the party that caused the injury owes a real and true debt to the one that they injured. The right of the injured party is to demand justice for their loss—an eye for an eye. They have a right to be restored. In the matter of forgiveness, the injured party gives up all rights to retributive justice in the matter of his loss.[1]

Further, forgiveness involves suffering, as does justice. In justice, the suffering is transferred to the party that caused the injury. They are made to suffer justly for what they have done or made to suffer wrongly in terms of malicious revenge that exceeds what the injured party has a right to execute. Forgiveness also involves suffering. To forgive, the injured party must decide to keep all the suffering of the loss to themselves and not ask that it be returned to the perpetrator.

Thus, forgiveness is not something that we do for ourselves, but something that we do solely as an act of mercy toward those to whom it is extended. The scoff attributed to Oscar Wilde that we ought to always forgive our enemies because nothing annoys them more is obviously something less than forgiveness. It is a form of revenge or at least a form of attempted justice. The same is true with harboring resentment when justice cannot be had immediately. Bitterness is only revenge waiting for opportunity.

We often mistake the perceived benefits of forgiveness with forgiveness itself. If you learn to forgive, will it lower your blood pressure and stress? It possibly will. Nevertheless, forgiveness is acting in a way in which we are giving up a right and not gaining a blessing. That is no different than the Darwinist view of forgiveness arising out of familial advantage. Gandhi said that forgiveness is an attribute of the strong.[2] However, if one forgives only for one's own sense of vainglory, then they are simply using the occasion of injury to push themselves up above the other. Pride is not forgiveness. Forgiveness is not us being the "bigger person" or seeing ourselves as thus. That too falls into the realm of attempted justice. Forgiveness, rather, is humbling to its giver.

What then is forgiveness in its true scriptural sense? Forgiveness is a selfless act of unnatural love of which fallen nature has no place. That is, mercy is not natural to the sinner in the state of their fallenness (i.e., the world of our experience). It offers no advantage to the giver of it (even if it may in their humility be turned into a blessing by God and others who see it). Therefore, when it is genuinely found, it cannot be explained in Darwinian terms or in fallen human reasoning. Forgiveness, if it exists at all, is

1. Note: This is not an act of governance but an individual act. Personal forgiveness does not negate the duty of governments to exact punishment. The state enacting punishment does not negate personal forgiveness.

2. Gandhi, *All Men Are Brothers*.

wholly selfless because it is giving up what is rightly one's own (i.e., justice). We must look for its example in the realms of supernatural grace and not nature. This is why the same ones who cry out, "Grace does not destroy nature," are also the ones who are ready to denigrate the practice of mercy. It is found apart from the fallenness of this world and is found in the grace of God's revelation. We must look for it in the mind and heart of God made known unto us. When forgiveness is truly practiced, it is not understood by the world which knows only its sinful selfishness. High-profile instances in which people from a Christian understanding have openly forgiven their enemies are maligned even by professing Christians as foolish. Mercy may be admired for various good and bad reasons, but it is rarely understood. It is no less than divine in its origin.

The origin of forgiveness can only be explained in reference to the personal God of the Scriptures. It is found in God's dealing with sinful men. It was or is divinely exercised in a real moral context of good and evil. There must be a wrong that has been done and a response from God to that wrong—transgression of the known law. It only fits biblical theism. A unitarian view of God cannot explain the origin of forgiveness. Only a God that can love can forgive. A unitarian god cannot explain the existence of any relational reality. Forgiveness derives from love. Islam or any Arian expression of deity cannot declare it. Only the God who is love can ultimately forgive in the advent of sin.

The first cause of forgiveness is God. It is a by-product of His nature as Creator. He is a God that gives humbly of Himself, to make Himself known to His creation. With the entrance of sin, the forgiveness of sin became a central part of redemption history. There was nothing that any man could do that could advantage God and earn forgiveness (see Ps 50). God forgives freely. One might ask, "Did He not demand sacrifices?" Yes, but not for His advantage—rather for man's advantage. The sacrifices commanded were not that God may be appeased, but to point in type to the provision He made. As Abraham learned, God will see to the matter Himself. God will provide Himself a Lamb (Gen 22:8). God did not excuse man's sin—rather He freely showed mercy by taking the injury upon Himself. We have forgiveness through the shedding of His blood (Eph 1:7).

Mercy is not condoning evil or wrongdoing. It is not an attempt to say that it was acceptable that the wrong happened. Forgiveness is not absent from judgment. It does not attempt to excuse the wrong by saying that there may have been extenuating circumstances that caused the wrong. Forgiveness sees evil as evil and does not attempt to do otherwise. It operates in a world of suffering, and it operates despite that world. The wrongdoer is not seen as anything less than morally responsible for their decisions.

When it comes to the sinner, this is the rub—they must see themselves as guilty and without excuse before forgiveness is made known. The publican saw himself as a sinner before he cried for the Lord to have mercy on him (Luke 18:13). The penitents see themselves in need of pardon. Penitents recognize that the wrong that they have done entitles the other to justice. All of this is cognizant for the giver of forgiveness as well. The pardon nulls the punishment. Forgiveness is the full extent of mercy. It is not simply lessening the punishment to something a little lighter, but the removing of the punishment altogether. Those who are asked to forgive sometimes fall into two separate traps. They falsely come to believe that forgiveness asks them not to see the wrong as wrong. Alternatively, they come to believe that forgiveness can still allow for some smaller punishment for the penitent.

The nature of forgiveness further necessitates reconciliation. Humanly speaking this is hard. We realize that the wrong that was done damaged the relationship between the wronged and the wrongdoer. Forgiveness longs for the restoration of that relationship. Any attempt to reconcile without forgiveness is to fail to fully reconcile. Bitterness will grow and trouble that relationship until it is destroyed (Heb 12:15).

There are instances in the present evil world where reconciliation is not possible. The unrepentant nature of the wrongdoer and the extreme level of risk posed by reconciliation are two such instances. Examples of this may be instances of child sexual abuse, extreme spousal abuse, or attempted murder. We should not forget that the Scriptures call for justice by the instrument of the state on behalf of the wronged or injured party when there is actionable injury. I can forgive the murderer of my child, but the state must still do its duty (Rom 13:1–8). In this sinful world, God has not necessitated the vulnerable to put themselves in the way of injury or to put others in their care in the way of injury. To seek legal remedies to address harm is not incongruent with forgiveness. One may seek those and still have a forgiving disposition. In such instances, it does become a matter of the heart. To forgive in those instances may be reduced to not carrying malice in the heart, not speaking ill, not hurling insults or merited curses, things that the perpetrator may rightly deserve. Such a measure of forgiveness may be the best one can do in the present evil world, when faced with such dire circumstances.

We must consider the forgiveness of Christ in all our musing. The candle that we light in our forgiveness is a lesser form of light compared to the brightness of the sun of His forgiveness. Forgiveness is a substantial and real thing. When we speak about the forgiveness of Christ, we are not speaking simply about Christ changing His feelings about us, or God the Father doing the same. There was a real debt of sin, a real wrong that we had done. It was a real accusation that was against us, and it was that thing that was forgiven by and through Christ. It was that real accusation that Christ took and nailed to His own cross. There was no resentment that Christ had to let go of. We stood with real guilt before a true and holy God that must judge our sin. Christ stood on our behalf and on behalf of the offended God to affect forgiveness and the full cancellation of that debt.

The true motive for forgiveness is divine. There is an emotional aspect of human forgiveness that is important to our experience. We carry resentment because our hearts are hardened by injury. Therefore, the releasing and relinquishing of resentment and bitterness become an effect of us forgiving. Nevertheless, Christ and the Father entered into the business of forgiveness without resentment. God so loved the world that He gave (John 3:16). He was the Lamb slain from the foundation of the world (Rev 13:8). That is the free mercy we are called to imitate. If we are to forgive like Christ, we must forgive out of a motive of love for those to whom we extend our forgiveness.

The forgiveness of Christ was simply not the act of forbearing punishment. God had been long-suffering to us before Christ affected our forgiveness. God is rich in mercy, because of the great love wherewith He loved us (Eph 2:4). All of salvation is the product of divine love. It is said of Christ that "God [hath] exalted [Christ] with his right hand to be a Prince and a Savior, for to give repentance to Israel, and forgiveness of sins" (Acts 5:31). All that the Father and Son had done, in that they so loved the world, was for the singular purpose of affecting our forgiveness. The apostles freely said that "through this man [Christ] is preached unto you the forgiveness of sins" (Acts 13:38).

When we consider the great love of Christ, we learn forgiveness. When He poured out His life's blood, for through that blood we may have the forgiveness of sin, we see forgiveness for what it truly is. Forgiveness is the perfect love of God (Eph 1:7). That divine love is beyond our understanding. We have the privilege of trying to know it to its fullest. We greatly seek to know the height, the width, the breadth, and the depth of that love (Eph 3:14–19). To be able to truly forgive is to first know that motive that drives forgiveness.

Again, forgiveness is free. This goes further than the motive. It goes to the method. The method speaks, largely, to the source of forgiveness. If forgiveness is freely given, then it is something that first comes from one that is absolutely free to give it. We are all indebted in some way. We need forgiveness just as much as we need to forgive. However, God is not such. We cannot accuse God of wrong. God is not indebted. Nevertheless, God is full of mercy and ready to forgive. Forgiveness is a product of free grace from one that has done no wrong. It comes from one that is without spot.

The power of forgiveness comes from pure holiness that can only be found in God. If this is not true, then true forgiveness cannot truly exist, but only a constant reciprocation of sinners passing judgment in hope of judgment passing from them. Forgiveness is such a pure thing that it must come from a pure source. Who can forgive sins but God? He alone can forgive freely. God alone occupies a place of perfect holiness, which is not compelled by conscience of guilt to spur to forgiveness. Forgiveness cannot be compelled in its purest sense.

Occupying a place of perfect holiness, God also occupies a place of perfect judgment. He alone can see the debt of sin for what it truly is. Further, occupying a place of perfect sovereignty, He alone fully is the party of the transgressed. It is always, when we sin, primarily God that is sinned against (Ps 51:4). God forgives sin. No one but God can forgive sin in an ultimate sense. This was the great controversy with Christ when He proclaimed that He, the Son of Man, had power on earth to forgive sins (Mark 2:5–11). He was, or rather is, holy, harmless, and free from sin, as well as made higher than the heavens (Heb 7:26). Thus, when He hung upon the cross, the forgiveness of God flowed from Him (Luke 23:34). Daniel rightly proclaimed of God, "To the Lord our God belong mercies and forgiveness" (Dan 9:9). When we freely receive Christ, we receive the source of all forgiveness. When we do, we find that the forgiveness that we offer is not ours at all, but His (Eph 4:32). Freely we received and freely we forgive (Matt 10:8). We become conduits of, and expressions of, the free grace and mercy of God to others.

Further, forgiveness is an expressed reality. "Jesus seeing their faith said unto the sick of the palsy; Son, be of good cheer; thy sins be forgiven thee" (Matt 9:2). Forgiveness is not simply something that is given, but something that is made known or revealed. For the injurious party to know their guilt but never know that the injured party had extended forgiveness is not forgiveness in its fullness. This goes beyond the idea that forgiveness is simply letting go of one's hurt. It must, by its very nature, be expressed to the other (if at all possible). The mercy of the Lord was not simply something that rested in His nature, but the Son, who is the Word of God, expressed it. The law came by Moses, but mercy and truth came by the Son (John 1:17).

There is something of the nature of forgiveness that demands the incarnation. Forgiveness was always intended to be a revealed thing. God made Himself known in the garden to sinful mankind, naked and in need, and gave promise. God declared in the law that He *shows* mercy to thousands that love Him (Exod 20:6). The poets and prophets expressed it in many ways. Last of all, God has spoken to us by His Son (Heb 1:1–3). It was He that declared that all manner of sin and blasphemy would be forgiven to men (Matt 12:31). Moreover, He expressed it at last from the pains of the cross. Any forgiveness that lacks expression, or that lacks revelation rather, is incomplete.

Forgiveness is an applied reality and not a legal fiction. In the Old Testament economy, the penitent would come to the priest who would offer sacrifices for the sinner and, based on the blood being applied to the altar, the sin would be forgiven. Forgiveness depends upon that ground in all its forms. Paul, when speaking of the justification of the sinner, quoted the psalmist, saying, "Blessed are they whose iniquities are forgiven, and whose sins are covered" (Rom 4:7). It is that covering of blood that satisfies the demand of justice of a Holy God. Forgiveness flows with the justice of God and not contrary to it. Paul again taught, "In whom we have redemption through his blood, the forgiveness of sins" (Eph 1:7). It is the basis of our spiritual life. "And you, being dead in your sins and the uncircumcision of your flesh, hath he quickened together with him, having forgiven you all trespasses" (Col 2:13). In addition, it is the basis of our continued fellowship with God and Christ: "If we confess our sins, he is faithful and just to forgive us our sins, and to cleanse us from all unrighteousness" (1 John 1:9). Divine forgiveness flows fully and wholly from the application of the substitutionary sacrifice. When it says to us that we forgive as Christ forgave us, or we forgive our debts as God has forgiven our debts, then the application of forgiveness must find the same basis (Eph 4:32; Matt 6:12).

The ground for forgiveness has already been applied. We find ourselves not needing to forgive others because of our own graciousness, but because of God's grace. We forgive because He forgives. That which covered us, and the deep blots that are against us, has the power to forgive them. If all manner of sin and blasphemy was forgiven you, then all manner of such may be forgiven them. This answers the hardest questions of whether we should forgive this or that egregious act committed against us. If we seek God to forgive our trespasses, then we are to forgive those that seek ours. We extend to others what is freely given to us.

In the matter of divine forgiveness, it is a permanent reality. We marvel at the connection that Christ often made to the permanence of forgiveness. He spoke to His disciples about forgiving seventy times seven when a brother turns to us to repent of a wrong (Matt 18:22). Man is apt to try to set limits, to say, "I will forgive only so much." However, the permanent nature of forgiveness flows supernaturally from its source, which is eternal and divine. Our God has said, "I will forgive their iniquity, and I will remember their sin no more" (Jer 31:34). God forgives all our trespasses. That divine forgiveness is meant to flow through us without limits. One of the points of the parable of Christ regarding the king that forgave a great debt to one who in turn failed to forgive a small debt to another was just that. The forgiveness of the great debtor was to encompass all debts owed to the great debtor as well (Matt 18:23–35). The permanency of the experience of our forgiveness should translate outward to those who stand in need of our forgiveness. This is the love of God, free and without limits to all who desire to enjoy it. God does not capriciously forgive to exact a debt again.

There are those who look at the doctrine of forgiveness and mock it. They say that such is fine for God, but it shows a lack of self-respect and self-esteem. Aristotle spoke of the need for appropriate anger in life to defend oneself from insult, and stated that all that were deficient in such were fools.[3] Hume taught that failing to feel resentment when wronged, as opposed to forgiveness, is a moral failing.[4] This seems to resonate with our baser nature. Such is the argument from nature. Nevertheless, it fails to see the Almighty and eternal nature that offers forgiveness, and it fails to see the great character of the love of God manifest in those who are conduits for such a divine nature.

3. Aristotle, *Nicomachean Ethics*.

4. Hume, *Treatise of Human Nature*.

If the character of God were ascertained, there would rarely be a need to discuss the appropriateness of forgiveness in most cases. There may be times that it is appropriate to be angry. There may be times that it is appropriate to escape. However, there are never times that it is appropriate to hold on to bitterness and an unforgiving spirit against those that seek our forgiveness. There is never an appropriate time for us to exact and harbor a sense of revenge. God has not done so to us and we cannot do so to others. To those who stand unrepentant of their wrong, we should still stand with a humbled heart ready to forgive as God does to the unrepentant sinner even now (Ps 86:5). To those who are unrepentant, we let justice and revenge lay in the hands of God alone (Rom 12:19).

That brings us to another point in this discussion: the necessity of forgiveness in the Christian life. The necessity of forgiveness lies first in our own fault. There is no man that does good and does not sin (Eccl 7:20). We must have a sense of our own sin when considering others. It affects our ability to approach God when we have wronged others. Our ability to bring our gifts to the altar of God is hindered until we make our sins right with those that we have wronged, or at least seek to make them right (Matt 5:23–24). Thus, Christ taught us that unless we forgive, or at least have the willingness to forgive, then we shall not be forgiven (Matt 6:14–15). There is no need for us to apply this to salvation.[5] It was to those born-again persons that called God "our Father" that Christ taught this thing, and He did not cease to be called the Father of those that fail.

Consider again the parable of the debtor. The debtor owed a great amount and, under the great sense of that debt and the punishment thereof, sought the forgiveness of that debt and gained it. He in turn went out and found one that owed him little, and when they sought him for forgiveness, he refused. For this, the wickedness of the debtor was revealed. The other servants saw it and went to their Lord who exacted the debt to the debtor. Then Christ said that it shall be thus with us if we refuse to forgive. We

5. To fail to forgive in the Christian life will result in us losing the sense of forgiveness in this life and not in the loss of salvation. Christ would later parse this when speaking of the "unforgivable sin," saying that there is forgiveness in this world and in the world to come. That permanence of unforgiveness is not added by Christ in cases of our failure to forgive. Salvation does not depend on our ability to do anything or in our performance of things we are able to do. Our salvation is all of grace. Therefore, to read the warning of Christ that we will lose forgiveness if we fail to forgive cannot mean the loss of salvation. It does yet mean something horrible: the loss of our sense of forgiveness and therefore our sense of fellowship with God. There is a need for us to forgive others as Christ forgave us.

cannot worship God rightly if we do not forgive, even when it is not possible to fully express it. "And when ye stand praying, forgive, if ye have ought against any: that your Father also which is in heaven may forgive you your trespasses" (Mark 11:25). We cannot stand in a right relationship with our brothers if we do not forgive. "Take heed to yourselves: If thy brother trespass against thee, rebuke him; and if he repent, forgive him" (Luke 17:3). This is the necessity that is laid upon those who follow Christ. To know Christ truly is to have a readiness to forgive.

In that, we find the principle of forgiveness. We forgive one another as Christ has forgiven us. The key to forgiveness, the full meaning thereof, lies in us being forgiven. Until that time, we cannot express forgiveness in any sense. Let that truth lie on the conscience of any who find themselves always demanding vengeance. The grandest need that we had was in our need of forgiveness. That was alone satisfied in Christ. All other needs of men toward us are encompassed and satisfied to us within that. When we experience that forgiveness, we open that tap.

We now know the blessed results of being forgiven. "Wherefore I say unto thee, her sins, which are many, are forgiven; for she loved much: but to whom little is forgiven, the same loveth little" (Luke 7:47). This is the outflow of love. It flows out toward those that suffer under sin, as we have. "So that contrariwise ye ought rather to forgive him, and comfort him, lest perhaps such a one should be swallowed up with overmuch sorrow" (2 Cor 2:7). Being that conduit, we help others find that love and forgiveness of Christ. "To whom ye forgive any thing, I forgive also: for if I forgave any thing, to whom I forgave it, for your sakes forgave it in the person of Christ" (2 Cor 2:10). This is the biblical impact of forgiveness. This is the life we are to live in Christ.

Bibliography

Aristotle. *The Nicomachean Ethics*. Translated by W. D. Ross and L. Brown. Oxford: Oxford University Press, 2009.

Baucham, Voddie T. Jr. *Fault Lines: The Social Justice Movement and Evangelicalism's Looming Catastrophe*. Washington, DC: Salem, 2021.

Bavinck, Herman. *The Origin, Essence, and Purpose of Man*. Fig Classic Series on Modern Theology. Kindle ed. San Fransisco: Fig, 2012.

Beckwith, Roger T. *The Old Testament Canon of the New Testament Church and Its Background in Early Judaism*. Grand Rapids: Eerdmans, 1986.

Bunyan, John. *The Holy War, Made by Shaddai Upon Diabolus, for the Regaining of the Metropolis of the World; Or, the Losing and Taking Again of the Town of Mansoul*. London: Newman, 1682.

Calvin, John. *Institutes of the Christian Religion*. Edited by John T. McNeill. Translated by Ford Lewis Battles. Louisville: Westminster John Knox, 1960.

Camus, Albert. *The Myth of Sisyphus*. Translated by Justin O'Brien. London: Penguin Classics, 2000.

Clark, Gordon H. *The Philosophy of Science and Belief in God*. Nutley, NJ: The Craig Press, 1964.

Dickens, Charles. *A Tale of Two Cities*. London: Penguin Classics, 2012.

Dostoevsky, Fyodor. *The Brothers Karamazov*. Translated by David McDuff. London: Penguin Classics, 2003.

Dumas, Alexandre. *The Count of Monte Cristo*. Ware, UK: Wordsworth Editions, 1997.

Ellicott, Charles John, et al. "James 2." In *Ellicott's Commentary for English Readers*, edited by Charles John Ellicott. London: Cassell and Company, 1905. https://biblehub.com/commentaries/ellicott/james/2.htm.

Frame, John M. *Theology in Three Dimensions: A Guide to Triperspectivalism and Its Significance*. Phillipsburg, NJ: P&R, 2017.

Gandhi, M. K. *All Men Are Brothers*. New York: Continuum, 1958.

Goodrick-Clarke, Nicholas. *Black Sun: Aryan Cults, Esoteric Nazism, and the Politics of Identity*. New York: New York University Press, 2002.

Hawking, Stephen. *A Brief History of Time*. New York: Bantam, 1989.

Heiser, Michael S. *The Unseen Realm: Recovering the Supernatural Worldview of the Bible*. Bellingham, WA: Lexham, 2015.

Henry, Matthew. "Romans 13." BibleHub. https://biblehub.com/commentaries/mhc/romans/13.htm.

Hume, David. *A Treatise of Human Nature*. Edited by L. A. Selby-Bigge. New York: Oxford University Press, 1958.

Johnson, Jeffrey D. *The Failure of Natural Theology: A Critical Appraisal of the Philosophical Theology of Thomas Aquinas*. Conway, AR: Free Grace, 2021.

Kant, Immanuel. *Critique of Pure Reason*. Translated by Paul Guyer and Allen W. Wood. Cambridge: Cambridge University Press, 1998.

Lewis, C. S. *The Weight of Glory and Other Addresses*. New York: HarperCollins, 2001.

Lyte, Henry Francis. "Abide with Me." Recorded November 1906. Library of Congress. Audio recording. https://www.loc.gov/item/jukebox-728378/.

Meyer, H. A. W. "James 2." In *Critical and Exegetical Commentary on the New Testament*, translated by W. P. Dickson. New York: Funk & Wagnalls, 1884. https://biblehub.com/commentaries/meyer/james/2.htm.

Michael, George. "David Lane and the Fourteen Words: Totalitarian Movements and Political Religions." *Politics, Religion & Ideology* 10 (2010) 43–61.

Pascal, Blaise. *Pascal's Pensées*. New York: E. P. Dutton, 1958.

Rousseau, Jean-Jacques. *The Social Contract*. Translated by Maurice Cranston. London: Penguin, 2004.

Schaeffer, Francis A. *The Church at the End of the Twentieth Century*. Downers Grove, IL: InterVarsity, 1970.

———. *Escape from Reason*. Downers Grove, IL: InterVarsity, 1968.

Singer, Peter. *Rethinking Life and Death: The Collapse of Our Traditional Ethics*. New York: St. Martin's, 1994.

Sowell, Thomas. *Discrimination and Disparities*. New York: Basic, 2019.

Spangler, Michael. *Christian Race Realism*. N.p.: Sacra, 2024.

Tackett, Jason. *Sex and the Gospel*. Eugene, OR: Resource, 2023.

Tolstoy, Leo. *Anna Karenina*. Kindle ed. New York: Norton, 1970.

Wallace, Daniel B. *Greek Grammar Beyond the Basics: An Exegetical Syntax of the New Testament*. Grand Rapids: Zondervan, 1996.

Waltke, Bruce K., and M. O'Connor. *An Introduction to Biblical Hebrew Syntax*. Winona Lake, IN: Eisenbrauns, 1990.

The Westminster Standard. "The Standards." https://thewestminsterstandard.org/the-westminster-standards/.

White, James, and Corey Mahler. "James White vs. Corey Mahler Debate Black Sanctification." Streamed live on May 15, 2025. YouTube video. Hosted by Bible Dingers. https://www.youtube.com/live/taMoR7aAz2Q?si=l8KMwR6uHItkIvao.

Wilde, Oscar. *The Picture of Dorian Gray*. Ware, UK: Wordsworth Classics, 1992.

Wolfe, Stephen. *The Case for Christian Nationalism*. Moscow, ID: Canon, 2022.

www.ingramcontent.com/pod-product-compliance
Lightning Source LLC
LaVergne TN
LVHW050645100826
845148LV00011B/1992

* 9 7 9 8 3 8 5 2 7 6 5 2 3 *